DIVERSITY IN HIGHER EDUCATION:

A WORK IN PROGRESS

Caryn McTighe Musil

With Mildred García, Yolanda T. Moses,
and Daryl G. Smith

With a Foreword by Paula P. Brownlee

An Evaluation Report on Nineteen Ford Foundation
Diversity Grantees at Residential Colleges and Universities

Association of American Colleges and Universities, 1995

Published by
Association of American Colleges and Universities
1818 R Street, NW
Washington, DC 20009

Copyright 1995

ISBN 0-911696-67-9
Library of Congress Catalog Card No. 95-80686

Contents

Foreword

The Association of American Colleges and Universities was delighted when the Ford Foundation invited us to consider publishing *Diversity in Higher Education: A Work in Progress.* Commissioned by the Ford Foundation, the report represents the work of four evaluators whose mandate was to assess the institutional impact of the first round of grants awarded under the Foundation's Campus Diversity Initiative to nineteen residential colleges and universities. The result is a document designed to assist academic institutions in thinking strategically and creatively about how to make diversity more integral to the mission and practices of higher education. Nothing could be more important to AAC&U at this historical juncture.

How to make full use of the profound educational opportunities before us of diversity both as a newly recognized force in American culture and as an historical fact in our shared human history around the globe has been a priority of AAC&U, especially in the last decade. The association's commitment and concern has been shown in projects like Engaging Cultural Legacies: Shaping Core Curricula in the Humanities, which involved sixty-three institutions from 1989 to 1993, the Program on the Status and Education on Women, a part of AAC&U's legacy since 1970, and most recently our ambitious initiative, American Commitments: Diversity, Democracy, and Liberal Learning, formally launched in January 1993. Through the American Commitments initiative, the association has worked directly with more than 120 institutions and involved more than eight hundred faculty and administrators.

It is in keeping with our larger mission as an association to continue to offer national leadership to our colleagues in higher education and engage with them in the important work of educating our students to be active, informed, productive participants in a pluralist society and an interdependent world. Critical to the success of such a task is mapping our progress and identifying areas inadequately addressed. The Ford evaluation report, *Diversity in Higher Education,* helps do just that.

By publishing this important and deliberately practical document, AAC&U hopes the report will be of value to the higher education community in its continuing engagement with diversity as a means of achieving educational excellence. As the report's title suggests, we are not at the end, but in the midst of *a work in progress*. Such a state is both exhilarating and at times a bit unsettling. AAC&U, however, welcomes the opportunity to join with you in that important construction project.

PAULA P. BROWNLEE

President, Association of American Colleges and Universities

Preface

Diversity and Higher Education: A Work in Progress is the collaboration of four authors who were selected by the Ford Foundation in the fall of 1992 to serve as an Evaluation Team to assess the first round of grantees in the Foundation's Campus Diversity Initiative. Instead of evaluating a series of nineteen discrete funded projects, the team decided to focus principally on a given project in terms of its impact on the institution as a whole. What difference did it make? Where might one turn for evidence? In what ways were the project's educational goals institutionalized to ensure an ongoing commitment to diversity?

The team also made clear from the beginning that we wanted to tease out from the multiple local campus experiences what lessons could be learned that might assist other campuses implementing their own diversity initiatives. We wanted practical, useful, proven advice from the field. Finally, given what emerged after the first generation of Ford Foundation diversity grants, we wanted to suggest future directions institutions might consider as they seek to create more inclusive communities.

All four members of the Ford Evaluation Team have had extensive experience in evaluation and have between us served in almost every area of campus life: as faculty members, academic administrators, and student affairs administrators. Each of us has been engaged in diversity issues in higher education for several decades, whether through scholarship, teaching, campus leadership, or some combination of all three. We have done our work at specific campuses but also through statewide activities, disciplinary and professional associations, and at the national policy level. Although the following report is informed specifically by the foundation's initial nineteen grant recipients in the Campus Diversity Initiative, the report is also influenced by the team's accumulated knowledge of diversity work in higher education across the country. The four team members include:

Mildred García, Ed.D.
Assistant Vice President for Academic Affairs
Montclair State University

Yolanda T. Moses, Ph.D.
President
The City College of the City University of New York

Caryn McTighe Musil, Ph.D.
Senior Research Associate
Association of American Colleges and Universities

Daryl G. Smith, Ph.D.
Faculty in Education and Psychology
The Claremont Graduate School

Although *Diversity in Higher Education* is the result of a genuinely collaborative effort by all four team members, Caryn McTighe Musil was the principal writer. She was responsible for turning notes, site reports, and conversations into a readable, coherent text. The other Evaluation Team members reviewed and edited drafts, adding new text where needed.

To gather data for the report, the Evaluation Team relied on a series of campus visits, conferences, team meetings, and information available in extensive files at the Ford Foundation from each participating grantee. During the course of the evaluation, the team was an observer-participant at three Ford Foundation conferences held for institutions that had received Ford diversity grants. The first Ford conference that the Evaluation Team attended was held in Pasadena, California, in September 1992; the second in Seattle, Washington, in October 1993; and the third in Tucson, Arizona, in October 1994.

In addition to meeting with Edgar Beckham, Ford's program officer overseeing the Campus Diversity Initiative, at the various Ford conferences, the team met with him at regular intervals to coordinate the evaluation. In January 1993, during the annual meeting of the Association of American Colleges and Universities, we all agreed on an evaluation strategy.

Supplementing the Ford diversity conferences for the grantees and the periodic team meetings, the four evaluators spent two days in March of 1993 reading extensive files at the Ford Foundation and drafting preliminary areas of investigation for site visits to serve as a working proposal for the Foundation. After the proposal was approved by the foundation in late May of 1993, the Evaluation Team visited twelve campuses during the course of the following six months. Most were two-day visits during which key administrative leaders, faculty, students, staff, and in some cases community representatives were interviewed.

In November 1994, at the national meeting of the Association for the Study of Higher Education (ASHE) in Pittsburgh, Pennsylvania, the Evaluation Team and Edgar Beckham presented a panel, Setting the Research Agenda for Diversity, based on preliminary discoveries. Following the ASHE meeting, President Yolanda Moses hosted a team meeting with Edgar Beckham at the City College to respond to an early draft version of the report and suggest revisions.

Since 1990, when the Ford Foundation announced the first round of grant awards, the number of institutions that have received grants under Ford's Campus Diversity Initiative has increased significantly. The foundation increased not only the number but also the kinds of institutions involved. The current profile of schools funded by Ford captures the diversity in higher education itself, which is so universally praised as a distinguishing national feature in the United States. There is now a wide variation in institutional size, type, and mission; in student demographics spanning age, economics, race, gender, and religion; and in geographic areas, both urban and rural, from across the country.

The current report, *Diversity in Higher Education*, however, is based only on the first nineteen grants awarded in the initial round. Although there is some diversity among them, these initial institutions were exclusively residential colleges and universities, most of which were liberal arts colleges. Our commentary is therefore grounded principally in the knowledge gleaned from that specific context. Although the Evaluation Team believes many insights, lessons, and principles that emerged will be applicable in many other contexts as well, we were fully aware that our sample did not represent the full spectrum of academic institutions found in higher education today. Undoubtedly, knowledge will be expanded and refined as additional evaluations emerge from the full range of institutions that have invested in diversity efforts. The Evaluation Team welcomes such studies.

Finally, all four team members are particularly indebted to the candor and generosity of the many students, faculty members, and administrators we met with over the course of the past two years. In their commitment and willingness to take risks lay our hope for more inclusive and enriched academic institutions. We are grateful as well to Edgar Beckham, whose probing questions, catalytic presence, and inspired leadership persuade so many people that the academy can, in fact, reconstitute itself if we have the will to do it and the vision to do it wisely.

Caryn McTighe Musil
August 1995

1 Introduction

[E]ducational democracy involves not only honoring other cultures in their unique integrity, but also working simultaneously with a diversity of human beings....We are all equal partners in a shared project of renegotiating the sense of belonging, inclusion, and full enfranchisement at our major institutions. Such renegotiations require time, patience, and careful listening.[1]

    Renato Rosaldo, *Culture and Truth: The Remaking of Social Analysis*

       This report is an attempt to capture some of the central lessons that emerged from nineteen residential colleges and universities that were recipients of Ford Foundation grants in the foundation's Campus Diversity Initiative. It is a story about institutional change, but institutional change that has at its core the still unresolved issue of inequalities and exclusions that haunt our nation and our campuses. The story of institutional change also has at its core the challenge to undo the habit of organizing knowledge and academic institutions around a single center. Instead, many campuses have begun—slowly but with increasing intellectual excitement—to displace a single, partial, and largely unchallenged center with multiple, expansive, and therefore necessarily contested centers. Each of them represents a beginning place, a standpoint from which initial perspective and knowledge is learned, and from which we can move to embrace increasingly fuller understandings of the lived reality of human existence.

       The story of institutional change on college campuses is also a narrative about tensions. Tensions that are rooted in impatience with marginality. Tensions rooted in resistance to making too many changes too fast. Tensions that are generative ones, ushering in intellectually compelling and institutionally transforming ways of seeing and organizing the worlds in

Newly empowered citizen groups
challenged the way society was
structured and the consequences of
those insistent voices reverberated
throughout higher education

---

which we live. And tensions that are destructive, driving people into hard-
ened, unexamined positions that function as fortified intellectual and social
bunkers hampering the creation of vibrant, inclusive communities. On
campus after campus, there is growing consensus that diversity must be attended to across race and class, gender and sexual orientation, religion and
ethnicity, and the seemingly endless variety that marks each of us in
multiple ways and which often governs the structures and policies of our
country and our campuses.

To resolve and respond to such tensions requires reevaluating structures of knowledge, patterns of relationships, and organizing principles of institutional life. The enterprise is exhilarating to some, deeply threatening to
others. But the transformation is well under way in colleges and universities.
The debates about the nature of those changes continue to rage on in the
public, but the campuses themselves are, for the most part, engaged in productive dialogue about how to build more inclusive institutions, how new
scholarship is redefining fields and opening up exciting new areas of investigation, and how students can better understand each other and negotiate
the boundaries of differences.

Diversity in Higher Education is divided into six chapters. The introduction, which offers an overview of the report, is followed by Chapter 2,
"The Social Context: From Fearful Divisiveness to a Vision of Community."
The latter seeks to provide an historical context for the Ford Foundation
initiative, poised as it was at the close of the twentieth century, yet antici-
pating the demands of the new millennium. The announcement of the
Campus Diversity Initiative in 1990 followed nearly a quarter of a century of
dramatic citizen action represented in the Civil Rights movement, peace
movement, and women's movement.

Newly empowered citizen groups challenged the way society was
structured and the consequences of those insistent voices reverberated
throughout higher education. All this was happening against a backdrop of
a massive reevaluation of education and its effectiveness in America. The
call to do things differently in academe was both embraced and resisted, and
there were profoundly different convictions about how to "fix" things. In

the mid-eighties, a fierce backlash to progress that white women and people of color in particular had achieved emerged in the form of a well-orchestrated critique of multiculturalism, which cast the drama being played out in starkly oppositional terms.

In the midst of this deeply contentious historical moment, the Ford Foundation sought to offer a new direction for higher education in hopes of generating alternative models of understanding, cooperation, and negotiation instead of what was increasingly becoming a model of polarization, rigidity, and attack. The foundation's involvement in these pressing societal issues was timely and influential. It both provided a vision and touched a resonant chord on campus. By awarding funds to institutions, the Ford Foundation validated the importance of a commitment to diversity, enhanced opportunities for innovative reforms, and hastened progress.

Chapter 3 of the report, "Diversity Initiatives: Toward a New Commonweal," turns to the inventive solutions of the nineteen Ford-funded residential colleges and universities. In an imaginative range of approaches, they created projects that led them to rethink structures and methods of their academic disciplines, design more inclusive curricula, address the needs of diverse student populations, and enrich the sense of community through understanding differences. The first part of Chapter 3 contains brief summary descriptions of the funded projects on each campus. The second part shifts from a campus-specific profile to a subject or thematic profile. Projects clustered in three main areas: faculty and curriculum development (by far the approach of choice), student-oriented projects, and research- and resource-focused projects.

The foundation's decision to invest the largest part of its grant money into faculty and curriculum development turned out to be a wise one. Although there was significant variety among the faculty development models chosen, the faculty members and therefore the future courses that will be taught to generations of students were visibly affected. Engaged intellectually with new questions, challenged to reconceive courses, and placed in dialogue with colleagues across many disciplines, faculty members became catalysts for reimagining the direction and scope of their institutions.

It is not surprising that fewer grants were submitted and awarded for student-oriented projects. As a transient population, students are thought to be risky if one is seeking lasting institutional change. In almost every instance, however, when students were the focus of a Ford-funded project on campus diversity, the results were—at least in the short run—quite impressive. Students demonstrated leadership, openness, and a new sense of empowerment as they became engaged in minority scholars programs, student-run cultural diversity festivals, and writing programs designed for first-year students.

Although fewer grantees opted to develop new resource materials, those that did produced valuable products. As such, they have a permanence to them and can be widely shared within a specific campus and sometimes even beyond those hallowed boundaries. In some cases, the resource material took the conventional but no less valuable form of new library resources, videos, and new diversity readers for English writing courses. In others, they moved diversity into new technologies, through such projects as computerized archival collections of African American culture and computerized mapping of all the diversity courses on a given campus.

While Chapter 3 analyzes the kinds of innovations within the funded projects themselves, Chapter 4 turns its attention to how projects affected the institution as a whole and how they were or were not sustained after external funds were depleted. Titled "Institutionalizing Project Goals and Planning Next Phases: Small Steps and Bold Visions," this section of the report relied upon three kinds of evidence to determine whether a project had a broader impact on an institution: (1) whether and how projects or their goals have become institutionalized; (2) the kind of internal and external networks that have emerged; and finally (3) the kind of assessment designs that could yield much needed data to evaluate the full impact of various grants over time.

In Chapter 4, the focus shifts from the descriptive and analytical one of the first three chapters to a more prescriptive one. In keeping with the thrust of the Ford evaluation mandate to discover what had been learned from several years of funded grants, the Ford Evaluation Team uses the chapter to lay out a blueprint of strategies that have proved especially effective in solidifying gains made by specific projects. The Chapter looks, therefore, at a range of ways to institutionalize diversity initiatives; the kinds of networks that sustain, expand, and enrich initiatives; and a series of questions that can be used to organize assessment designs. Assessment is essential in evaluating the institutional impact of diversity work, student learning in diversity courses, and the kind of community that characterizes campus life. The Evaluation Team found the nineteen campuses rich in ideas for institutionalizing diversity, creative—for the most part—in establishing ongoing networks, but with few exceptions, surprisingly bereft of significant data that could evaluate the impact of their specific diversity project.

In a continuum with the preceding section, Chapter 5 is called "Lessons Learned, or I Wish I Had Thought of This Before I Started." Although its advice-column clustering is grounded in lessons learned from evaluating the nineteen Ford-funded initial grantees, the insights are also informed by the reflections of the Evaluation Team itself through its collective sense of what the team members have learned over the years from an ever-widening sampling of projects. "Lessons Learned" assumes as its audience not so much those who have already completed diversity projects, but rather those just beginning them. Its purpose, then, is to function as a pithy collection of the accrued wisdom amassed at this juncture. It moves from considering how to build consensus, maximize a grant's impact, and structure it to how to engage faculty, rethink the curriculum, secure financial and administrative support, and generate diversity initiatives within student affairs.

The final chapter, "Implications for the Next Generation of Diversity Projects," offers some parting insights with an eye to the next level of understanding in light of the complexity of the task as well as its compelling intellectual and social justice questions. How might academia fold in the knowledge gained about diversity from past projects into the new efforts to redesign and improve the quality of education in the academy? The stories from the field are inspiring ones, bold ones, and sometimes failed ones. We all can learn something from them. In that spirit, the team offers an evaluation of those committed efforts.

2 The Social Context: From Fearful Divisiveness to a Vision of Community

When those who have the power to name and to socially construct reality choose not to see you or hear you, whether you are dark-skinned, old, disabled, female, or speak with a different accent or dialect than theirs, when someone with the authority of a teacher, say, describes the world and you are not in it, there is a moment of psychic disequilibrium, as if you looked into a mirror and saw nothing.[2]

Adrienne Rich, *The Feminist Classroom*

The Ford Foundation Campus Diversity Initiative was formally announced February 8, 1990. It is no accident that it was issued at the beginning of the last decade of the twentieth century. Standing on the edge of two decades, the Ford Foundation initiative was profoundly shaped by the events of the quarter of a century that immediately preceded its announcement. It offered a visionary challenge for higher education to look ahead to the next quarter of a century to, in effect, reinvent itself to meet the needs of the twenty-first century. The foundation took a stand by defining one of the central issues for the academy in the United States at this historical juncture: "building the capacity to accept and thrive upon intellectual and human diversity." Diversity itself, however, was seen in the context of community both local, national, and global and as a matter of citizenship. "To limit diversity within the commonwealth is stultifying," asserted the open letter signed by seven college and university presidents, the director of the American Council on Education's Office of Minority Concerns, the president of the College Board, and the President of the Ford Foundation. "To pursue diversity without regard for the commonwealth can lead to anarchy," they insisted.[3]

By the end of the eighties, the majority
of undergraduates were female, and
white women and people of color made
up 60 percent of undergraduate and
masters degree recipients

What propelled the foundation and presidents of universities and colleges to such a point? The answer lies, in part, in the period of dramatic changes in American society during the preceding quarter of a century and in the educational reform movement of the eighties. The GI Bill in postwar America had opened higher education in America to 2.5 million men— and a few women—whose age, ethnicity, race, and class would have been barriers to most of them before the war. Following in their footsteps, as a result not of war but of two powerful social movements, the Civil Rights movement and the women's movement, people of color and white women benefitted from new access to education in the late sixties and seventies. By the end of the eighties, the majority of undergraduates were female, and white women and people of color made up 60 percent of undergraduate and masters degree recipients.

Although the period leading up to the eighties was characterized by enhancing equal access to education for formerly restricted or excluded populations, the eighties were characterized by a vocal public debate about the quality of education. Some argued that there was a direct correlation between the new populations, the democratization of the governance of higher education, and the decline in quality. Others, also concerned about improving the quality of education, ascribed the decline to other institutional factors, such as campus climate, teaching effectiveness, and resource limitations and expectations. But in the early eighties, all joined in the clarion call for educational reform. During the course of the decade, however, there was heated and sometimes acrimonious debate about to what ends, for whom, and how reforms were enacted. In *The Closing of the American Mind*, Allan Bloom argued that higher education had lost its way when it abandoned its proud academic tradition of the fifties. "[I]n 1955," Bloom claimed, "no universities were better than the best American universities in the things that have to do with a liberal education and arousing in students the awareness of their intellectual needs."[4] Others at the heart of the reform movement offered a different remedy. They thought the solution lay not in recreating institutions of exclusion from the fifties when there was de jure and de facto racial segregation, quotas on Jews, closeted homosexuals, repressive policies against free political expression, and the lowest percentage of women in higher education since the twenties. Rather, these reformers argued, the solution lay in creating institutions of inclusion.

By the end of the eighties, in some states the changes in demographics were driving academic institutions toward diverse student populations whether they sought it or not. In states like California, Texas, Florida, New York, and New Jersey, new national immigration laws had dramatically increased the number of people of color within their borders. By 1987, less than 25 percent of the freshman class at Berkeley were white men and there was no longer any majority population. In other states with more homogenous populations but mobile national and international workforces, the fact that the workplace would be more diverse than ever was a compelling reason for many institutions to rethink what kind of educational preparation their students needed to succeed in such a changed environment.

If social and political forces altered the composition of the potential pool of undergraduate students, intellectual forces altered the landscape of academic scholarship. For more than two decades, the new scholarship on women, racial minorities, and ethnic groups gradually accumulated to such a point that it could no longer be ignored or dismissed as tangential. During the last decade, lesbian and gay studies, Jewish studies, as well as new scholarship about age, disability, and non-Western culture joined with the other new scholarship to pose the most significant challenge to the structures of traditional knowledge since the Renaissance. Few disciplines remained unaffected. Disciplinary associations, the boundaries and assumptions of departmental structures, commonly understood paradigms, the kinds of courses offered, and the foci of research, were all influenced by the weight and compelling revelations of the new scholarship on formerly excluded subjects.

For many, the old methods of organizing knowledge were no longer sufficient. On some campuses there were, in fact, more interdisciplinary programs than traditional majors. Traditional knowledge structures proved themselves incapable of containing the new intellectual areas of exploration. Former departmental arrangements proved inadequate in solving social and intellectual issues that were at heart interdisciplinary.

If faculty were principally concerned with the challenges the new scholarship posed, students were principally concerned about their daily lives on campus. Bernice Sandler's paper, *Chilly Climate for Women in the Classroom*,[5] (written in 1984 for the Association of American Colleges) coined the term *chilly climate*. It soon became a catch phrase that captured the notion that learning occurs in a context, an environment that can enhance growth or stifle it. Research data supported claims that access was just the first step toward equality. A second step was creating equal treatment after one walked through the newly opened door. There was, then, a period of reform on many campuses that heeded questions of climate by instigating sexual harassment policies, racial harassment policies, speech codes, resident life programs, freshman orientation, and other mechanisms that could contribute to creating a climate where previously excluded populations could thrive and not merely survive.

For some on campus, all these changes in the scholarship, curriculum, student life, and student constituents were unsettling. The changes felt threatening and the evolving world of higher education increasingly unfamiliar. In some cases, those who had originally supported new access to education for many populations were not prepared to change the nature of their institution. Instead, they wanted the new students to fit into what was already there. When that didn't happen and the institution itself began ever so slowly to change, some felt a sense of loss or resentment. A few were bristling defensively from being displaced from the center of the educational enterprise.

Though small in numbers, the critics of multiculturalism were very successful in defining for the media the issues as they saw them. In most cases, however, the picture painted distorted the actual work going on in colleges and universities. While the media covered the canon war debate as if it were only that—faculty at loggerheads over what should be taught—faculty members around the country had long been voluntarily changing their curriculum to include new subject areas based on the new scholarship. By the time Stanford University, in the late eighties, had made its rather modest but much discussed alteration in their introduction to Western civilization course, they were not a pacesetter as the media portrayed them, but instead lagged behind the curriculum transformations at hundreds of other institutions.

Always reinvigorated when a controversy was imminent, the media then moved in syncopated frenzy from covering the canon wars to uncovering what they determined was the real hidden crime undermining higher education: political correctness. *PC* became synonymous in many people's minds with any reform effort. Concerted efforts to change a system that had not met everyone's needs were smeared as being political indoctrination. By contrast, concerted efforts to defend the status quo were lauded as a neutral guardianship of the academy's most sacred values.

While faculty and administrators debated canons and speech codes, unresolved social problems began to tear at the fabric of the nation. By the end of the eighties, public attention became preoccupied with violence in the inner cities, a recession that hit middle-income families as well as the poor, high unemployment especially among minority populations, teen pregnancies, drugs, and disturbing evidence that the United States had become sharply divided economically into two nations: one rich and one poor. One out of three children lived below the poverty line, the vast majority of whom were minority children. The organized movement for gay and lesbian rights galvanized with intensity as AIDS inflamed homophobia. Immigrants streamed into the United States from Central America as people were driven out by wars and terrorism; others crossed the Mexican border because of the promise of greater economic opportunities in the United States. Within much of the black community, a new militancy emerged and Malcolm posters replaced or stood beside Martin. Within many of our city neighborhoods, new violent instances exploded revealing deep and recurring racial, ethnic, and religious animosities. Birth control clinics were scenes of terrorist attacks, and in alarming numbers women continued to be victims of violence by men.

It became more difficult for any academic institution to isolate itself from these issues. Students carried the realities with them onto the campuses like books in their backpacks. During the eighties, there was also a devastating withdrawal of federal funds from higher education, which changed the

Diversity ought to be woven into the academic
life and purpose of the institution....Our world
is pluralistic and education cannot responsibly
turn its back upon that reality

nineties from what was to be the decade of the new generation of young faculty to the decade of downsizing, minimal turnover in faculty, and painfully
restricted budgets. Outright grants to students shrank, and the desire to re-
cruit a more diverse student body collided with economic restraints. Many
students of color felt resentment that just as they were entering the academy,
new access possibilities were narrowing rather than expanding.

It was in this context that the Ford Foundation sought to provide
direction, vision, and a source of values. It challenged higher education "to
embrace the rich diversity of American life in a manner that enhances the
educational experiences of all students."[6] It argued that diversity would become a means of reassessing the purposes and practices of higher education.
Ford posited that rather than being a divisive force, diversity may ultimately
prove to be a unifying one. Through its Campus Diversity Initiative, the
Ford Foundation saw the possibility of linking the three streams of what
seemed to be competing sources of influence. The first was the educational
reform movement that argued for greater access, a redefinition of higher education's societal obligations, widening the areas of scholarship, and transformation of the curriculum and campus life. The second was the educational reform movement that argued for higher academic standards, the
depoliticization of campus life, the preservation of older, more mainstream
western traditions, and the validation of individual rights as the principal
means to achieve social justice. Swirling around both of these seemingly
oppositional forces were the unresolved social tensions that spilled onto
campuses and into classroom dynamics.

Through its initiative, the Ford Foundation saw diversity as a way to
meet the concerns of all three and insisted there was room for dialogue and
common remedies. "Diversity ought," the public statement read,

> to be woven into the academic life and purpose of the institution:
> valued by faculty, expressed through the curriculum, sustained and
> nourished through cultural expression and extracurricular life.
> Moreover, diversity of opinions must be protected against even the
> best intentioned constraints. Our world is pluralistic and education
> cannot responsibly turn its back upon that reality.

The foundation's initiative legitimized the importance of diversity as a central educational mission and of race relations as unfinished business in American democracy. In offering financial support, Ford challenged schools to be creative and thoughtful about how best to review their goals and purposes as they linked diversity to quality.

3 Diversity Initiatives: Toward a New Commonweal

[T]his world is fragile. The word he chose to express "fragile" was filled with the intricacies of a continuing process, and with a strength inherent in spider webs woven across paths....It took a long time to explain the fragility and intricacy because no word exists alone, and the reason for choosing each word had to be explained....That was the responsibility that went with being human...the story behind each word must be told so there could be no mistake in the meaning of what had been said; and this demanded great patience and love.[7]

Leslie Marmon Silko, *Ceremony*

Although the Ford initiative was launched in stages over the years from 1990 to 1994, the first phase was directed at "undergraduate education in the arts and sciences in largely or wholly residential institutions." Two hundred institutions were invited to submit proposals of two kinds: a grant of up to one hundred thousand dollars to pilot a new project over a two-year period, or a grant of up to twenty-five thousand dollars to expand or enhance an existing effort.

There were four general criteria for proposals. Reviewers looked for evidence of a collaborative effort and commitment by faculty, students, and administrators; the relationship between earlier institutional diversity efforts and the proposed one; the centrality of the project to the institution's overall academic purpose; and evidence that the institution was prepared to support the project with its own resources during its duration and continue it in an appropriate form after the external funding was depleted. It was important to the success of the project that each institution had control over defining how to approach diversity, what its own institutional priorities were, what was appropriate for it given its mission, and what the most strategic steps to take were at this particular point in their institution's history.

Out of the glare of the media, which was at first a blessed relief, a number of colleges and universities began to build the kind of consensus and commitment necessary to meet Ford's challenges. The hard, unflashy labor of reform took place in committee meetings, libraries, and at computers; in classrooms, student programming, and across the table from local community leaders. The aggregate small actions ultimately created a new landscape of reform and possibilities.

On September 12, 1990, the first recipients of the Ford diversity initiative were formally announced, and it is these projects at largely residential colleges and universities that are the focus of this report. The nineteen institutions receiving grants included

> Bemidji State University
> Boston College
> Brandeis University
> University of California–Los Angeles
> Denison University
> Haverford College
> University of Iowa
> Millsaps College
> Mount St. Mary's College
> New School for Social Research
> University of Notre Dame
> Pitzer College
> University of Redlands
> University of Rochester
> Southwest Texas State University
> Spring Hill College
> Tulane University
> Virginia Commonwealth University
> Wesleyan University

Among the institutions there was an enormous variety of creative and thoughtful approaches to engaging diversity. The vast majority fell into two major but related categories. The first put primary focus on faculty development as a starting point; the second focused instead on a specific course or set of courses. The former began by introducing faculty to the new scholarship on diversity, typically done through seminars, workshops, and colloquia of varying lengths and intensities. From such larger, usually interdisciplinary frameworks, a faculty participant was then responsible for doing the necessary translation within his or her own discipline in order to create or alter a specific course. In the approach used by more than half of the grantees, faculty members proposed from the very start to modify or create a particular course and sought time to do the necessary study, usually alone and within disciplinary boundaries, to rethink the course. Even though the starting place differed in each approach, the goal ultimately was to enhance the curriculum, and in each case, to do so faculty members needed adequate time to read the new scholarship on diversity. Although never the central organizing principle of any of the nineteen submitted proposals, the relationship of pedagogy to diversity was addressed in about 20 percent of the projects, always in the context of the curriculum and faculty development proposals.

Two other significant strategies chosen by grant recipients looked to students as the point of departure rather than faculty. About one-quarter to one-third of the grantees opted for this approach either in concert with or independent of faculty and curriculum development. The first of these two strategies for engaging diversity involved student-centered projects in which student affairs took the lead. These ran the gamut from student-run workshops on cultural differences to minigrants to student groups, from freshman orientation programs to student internships and student debate series. The second of these student-centered strategies was centered in academic rather than student affairs but represented a spectrum of innovative ways to foster student-faculty research teams. Most of these teams paired faculty with students to create and revise courses, but a few used this approach to conduct field research or individual research projects.

Although few chose this as a single strategy, more than one-quarter of the grantees used cultural events as a vehicle for promoting diversity. These included week-long festivities, a series of cocurricular activities spread throughout the academic year, and special links with cultural institutions and resources in local communities. Still others focused on developing research or resource materials: one opted to create a new freshman anthology for a course required of all students; another created a computer program that mapped existing diversity courses for students; and a third established an impressive archival collection of black history in Richmond, Virginia. The latter project was one of three that deliberately sought links with the community as a means of enhancing understandings of diversity on their campuses.

DESCRIPTIONS OF THE NINETEEN GRANT PROJECTS

The following summary descriptions are just that: abbreviated versions of what were complex and multilayered project designs. They can only begin to suggest the contours of experimentation and careful thought that are represented by these nineteen institutions. Nonetheless, the Evaluation Team thought it would be useful for readers to have some indication of the variety, imaginativeness, and shrewdly crafted approaches to integrating diversity more completely into the intellectual, social, and organizational life of the academy.

Bemidji State University. The main thrust behind the Bemidji project entitled Enlarging Our Vision: Celebrating Diversity within a Common Heritage was to encourage the faculty at both Bemidji and the Arrowhead Community College System to develop multicultural, gender, and/or Native American materials for their courses. In order to prepare the faculty for this endeavor, four daylong symposia were held that explored the issue of cultural diversity. Two of the four symposia were held on the Native American reservations. Bemidji, which is surrounded by four Native American reservations, developed a process whereby minigrants were awarded to faculty to develop the curriculum materials. By the end of the grant, twenty-nine projects were funded: eight to faculty from Arrowhead Community College and the rest to the faculty at Bemidji.

Boston College. There were three main components to Boston College's Cultural Diversity Project: (1) faculty and curriculum development; (2) the Benjamin Mays Mentoring Program; and (3) research on and programming about racial attitudes on campus. The heart of the faculty and curriculum development involved summer grants awarded to six clusters of faculty developing courses with a strong multicultural emphasis designed to fulfill core requirements. With initial funds from the Ford Foundation, two five-day summer institutes were organized to train a cadre of advisors who could then train others in mentoring skills so faculty could better meet the needs of minority students at the college. By the grant's end, more than 50 faculty were actively engaged as mentors to more than 150 students enrolled in the Benjamin Mays Mentoring Program. The final component has evolved into a long-range research project that will examine the climate at Boston College in order to determine what remedies are needed to develop a healthier atmosphere for students of color and white students.

Brandeis University. This project involved a five-week Faculty Development Summer Seminar directed at faculty, both full and part time, both junior and senior, who taught what was a required two-semester humanities course. The first semester focused on literature of antiquity; the second began in the Middle Ages and continued into the twentieth century. The Summer Seminar introduced participants to the scholarship on Africa and African American culture so each could revise both semester courses in light of a more comparative and integrated approach. Although the revised courses were taught for two years after the Ford grant, a new curriculum was adopted in which the two-semester humanities courses were essentially eliminated in favor of a new set of freshman seminars dispersed and individualized in many different departments. Some of the "old" but newly revised humanities courses can be offered as freshman seminars, but faculty members from the Ford-funded Summer Seminar are seeking to invent new curricular space for the new knowledge they gained through the seminar.

University of California–Los Angeles. UCLA's Ford grant sought to develop a curriculum more reflective of the heterogeneity of Southern California and to design complementary cultural programs. There were four components to the project. The first created a large multidisciplinary core lecture course entitled "American Culture and Aesthetic Values." The second supported eight student seminars that focused on a variety of ethnic art forms, particularly those currently practiced in the Los Angeles area. The third component established a lecture series, "Ethnic Los Angeles," that was open to the public and examined the multicultural riches of the city through its architecture, monuments, and street art. The fourth and final component sought to coordinate on-campus and off-campus cultural events to promote interchange and mutual appreciation.

Denison University. The current Ford grant was intended to build on the work of the last ten years at Denison University to develop courses that satisfy the multicultural requirement (known as the J Requirement). After having completed a review of the curriculum, the former dean of the College saw that the courses that satisfied the J Requirement were being filled by upper-class students so that freshmen and sophomores were not being exposed to these issues. The Ford grant made it possible for faculty members to design and redesign courses that were part of the Freshman Studies Program to include issues of diversity. The Freshman Studies Program consists of two required courses: one is a semester course, "Words and Ideas," which focuses on writing and is largely taught by the English department; the second is a semester set of courses from which students choose a topic of interest. Through faculty summer workshops and course development grants, courses were redesigned so that significant portions of the first-year class could take at least one, and possibly two, such courses that included a focus on diversity.

Haverford College. The Ford grant was structured to support two interdisciplinary faculty seminars, one in spring 1991 and the second in 1992, for faculty who were developing new or revised courses to meet a new Social Justice Requirement that was passed at the same moment Haverford was applying for the Ford grant. Replacing the 1984 Diversity Requirement, the new Social Justice Requirement allows students to take a course that focuses on one or both of the following: (1) the nature, workings, and consequences of prejudice and discrimination, including those that arise from confrontations with radical difference, otherness, or foreignness; and/or (2) efforts at social and cultural change directed against and cultural achievements that overcome prejudice and discrimination. Each year, eight faculty members were selected from applicants and given either a stipend or a reduced schedule so they could meet for two hours every week in self-guided seminar discussions. They opted for interdisciplinary general readings in common for the first half and then in the second half moved to readings of specific works for each of their respective areas of investigation.

University of Iowa. There were four separate programs initiated through the Ford grant at the University of Iowa: (1) the development of *The Rhetorical Reader* through the Department of Rhetoric; (2) a series of supplemental resources and training programs for English department faculty members who teach "Interpretation of Literature," a required general education course; (3) a series of four debates sponsored by the University of Iowa Forensic Union; and (4) a series of three separate faculty seminars, each of which met six times over the course of an academic year. In the first program, a group created a new anthology offered on a voluntary basis that included more voices of people of color. A diversity task force within the English department's General Education Program sought to widen the titles in a required course and produced two resource supplements for teachers: *Contexts Resource Guide* with annotated syllabi and appended bibliographies of secondary sources and *Teaching Differences: Five Perspectives in Multiculturalism in the Literature Class*, which focuses on pedagogy.

Millsaps College. Millsaps College, located in Jackson, Mississippi, chose to use its Ford grant to expand knowledge on its campus about African American culture. It did this by awarding summer grants to faculty members to develop new courses, allocating funds to the library for acquisitions in this area, and giving stipends to undergraduate students for research projects that drew upon the resources of the local black community. In particular, students used the rich collection and archives of the Smith-Robertson Museum and Culture Center in Jackson, which specializes in African American culture and art.

Mount St. Mary's College. The Ford grant was structured for three purposes: to develop a weekend college, to infuse the core curriculum with multicultural perspectives, and to develop an assessment program. The most significant element, from the college's perspective, was the general education infusion project. The curricular infusion project centered on a series of Friday workshops in which faculty members from the college and outsiders introduced resources, curricular approaches, and new pedagogical possibilities. In addition to stipends for workshop attendance, funds were used to provide opportunities for summer projects and travel to conferences. The primary emphasis at this time seems to be the introduction of culture-specific perspectives such as Latin America and Africa and cross-cultural perspectives throughout the curriculum using a philosophy of "infusion and inclusion." The Ford project, in combination with other grant funds, has incorporated the library staff and library materials as a key element in improving curricular resources. Significantly, student affairs staff members have also been included in the activities of the project. Along with numerous impressive monographs on diversity, Mount St. Mary's has developed a sophisticated model of student outcome assessment.

New School for Social Research. Using a faculty-student collaborative model, the New School for Social Research's Ford-funded project, Creating a Diverse Curriculum, sought to create or transform courses at either the first-year level or in "orienting" courses within areas of concentration. Through a series of competitive summer stipends, selected faculty members worked with students to generate new courses. Several of the newly created courses were linked with another major program, the High Schools Collaborative Program, to create a teacher-to-teacher collaboration between New York City high schools and the New School's Eugene Lang College. They also organized a series of activities for faculty members on interpersonal relations and pedagogy that included outside speakers, discussions, and readings.

University of Notre Dame. Notre Dame's Ford grant supported a two-week intensive conference on curricular revision for about fifty members of the faculty, most of whom teach either in the University's Freshman Writing and Seminar Program or in the Sophomore Core Course. Faculty members were expected to make course revisions based on new knowledge gained through the workshops. Two bibliographers in the sciences and humanities also developed resources—both audiovisual and written—to support curricular revisions by faculty members. Portions of the seminar were videotaped to serve as a guide for future conferences as well as to orient new and adjunct faculty.

Pitzer College. The Ford grant included three major components: curriculum transformation, a community leadership series, and internships. The curriculum transformation element was designed to introduce more diversity into the curriculum through a series of interdisciplinary faculty seminars. The goal of the seminars was to encourage course redesign particularly for introductory courses intended to "decenter" the curriculum, looking at major issues from perspectives not normally included. Over the two-year period, eight seminars were held involving *two-thirds* of the Pitzer faculty, a stunning percentage. The faculty members received stipends and a small allowance for photocopying relevant materials. The second part of the project, community leadership, established more links with the Los Angeles community by bringing speakers to the campus. Seven events were held on topics ranging from a conference on women's work to a workshop on the medical and cultural needs of American Indians. The third component of the grant supported a community internship program through the hiring of an internship coordinator who succeeded in making connections to a wide range of community organizations.

University of Redlands. The University of Redlands focused its grant on increasing awareness of how cultural differences influence ways of thinking and acting. To accomplish this they designed a series of activities for faculty, student affairs personnel, and students. Activities for faculty included a four-week workshop to introduce cultural diversity into the curriculum and a special focus at the annual faculty retreat. Two-day workshops on intercultural understanding in residential life and social settings were also organized for student affairs staff and faculty members advising student groups. Student government leaders were encouraged to sponsor programs highlighting cultural diversity, which resulted in a very successful festival, Living on Common Ground, which has grown every year.

The University of Rochester. The University of Rochester developed a four-part initiative: two involved course development, one was directed towards faculty development, and the fourth awarded senior research grants on cultural diversity and race relations. The first of the curriculum initiatives developed new courses to enhance an existing freshman sequence, Ourselves and Others: Cultural Diversity in the Modern World. The second developed new courses for the junior seminar series focusing on cultural diversity. Through the Faculty Colloquium on Cultural Diversity, two dozen faculty members from seven departments met on a regular basis for discussions and lectures and were influential in shaping the junior seminars on diversity and the senior research awards.

Southwest Texas State University. Southwest Texas State University's project, Exploring the Southwest: In Search of Community, distinguished itself by being so student-centered. Through curricular development, public cultural celebrations, and discussions in the residence halls, the project aimed to introduce students to the multicultural heritage of the American Southwest. In the curricular component, students worked with faculty members to develop materials for a course on Spanish dialects of Texas and learned fieldwork techniques so they could study two southwestern communities. The week of festivities celebrating sixteenth-century explorer, Cabeza de Vaca, focused on early patterns of multiculturalism in the coming together, both in conflict and cooperation, of Spanish, African, and Native American cultures in the New World. A portion of the grant was also used by the Center for Multicultural and Gender Studies to conduct a series of faculty and curriculum development workshops that assisted faculty members in transforming a current course or designing a new one, thus increasing the number of "Cultural Pluralism Emphasis" courses.

Spring Hill College. This project had two main components. The first was to provide support to diverse students through the creation of a Multicultural Office, and the second was to begin the process of infusing diversity into the curriculum through interdisciplinary teaching. By the end of the grant, the Multicultural Office had become a transforming force on campus, and a Multicultural Student Union had been formed. To infuse diversity into the curriculum, Spring Hill opted to create teams of three to four faculty members who studied the new scholarship in a given area, created new diversity courses for the sophomore curriculum, and team-taught the new course the first time it was offered. Spring Hill also used grant money to enhance the library resources on diversity.

Tulane University. Because the curriculum lagged behind other more visible signs of campus diversification, Tulane chose to design a project where two-thirds of the funds went toward faculty development and the creation of new diversity courses. They did, however, opt for a multiple approach to diversity by having three major parts to their proposal: summer stipends over two years for faculty members, along with funds to bring in speakers to reach a larger proportion of faculty; summer research scholarships for minority students under the guidance of a faculty mentor; and minigrants for student organizations. The initiative was called Advancing Cultural, Sexual, and Ethnic Plurality at Tulane (ACSEPT). They awarded each of ten faculty members a $3,000 stipend each summer to develop a new course and attend a two-hour seminar with colleagues for four weeks during the summer. Summer awards of $2,000 each to six minority students during each of the two summers of the grant were made in which each student had to write a directed research proposal in the area of their intended major and do so under faculty supervision. Although fewer student organizations applied for the minigrants than expected, several awards were made to groups for projects that promoted new understandings about diversity.

Virginia Commonwealth University. The centerpiece of Virginia Commonwealth's project was the creation of the Black History Archives Project. The establishment of the archives provided the formation of a database that documents many aspects of the several hundred-year-old black community in the Richmond area where Virginia Commonwealth University is located. Through this project, the black community became part of the campus, faculty were able to use the information to enhance their cur-

The evaluation highlighted that one cannot
improve and rethink the curriculum without
offering opportunities for faculty members to
rethink what they know

---

riculum, and students had access to a community they were typically unfamiliar with. VCU developed a video featuring black leaders in Richmond in
order to convince those outside of the city to become part of the Black History Archives Project. They currently hope to work with community groups
in Norfolk to add archives from that city's black community to Virginia
Commonwealth's Library Collection. Long-range plans include connecting
the project to the world through Internet.

Wesleyan University. To increase the number of diversity courses
and give visibility to courses already being offered, Wesleyan used its Ford
grant in three ways: to fund (1) a series of grants to faculty to create new
and revised courses; (2) presentations from Wesleyan faculty as well as from
outside scholars to expand campuswide interest in multiculturalism; and (3)
a user-friendly computer program that mapped the vast array of diversity
courses already in place. The third strategy became the focal part of the
grant and eventually went far beyond the imagined impact of its creators.
The computer mapping project clustered courses around a theme, topic, or
geographic area so students could more easily see conceptually related diversity courses and devise an individualized, coherent program of study accordingly. The success of mapping diversity courses through the computer, however, was so striking that other departments quickly understood the
possibilities inherent in the program to bring similar intellectual coherence
to other disciplinary areas. What had begun, then, as a mapping project for
diversity courses at Wesleyan has now evolved into a project to map much
of Wesleyan's entire curriculum. It has also spawned a new computer program called *Diversity Connections*, which is mapping diversity offerings
nationally and will be offered to the public in 1996.

FACULTY AND CURRICULUM DEVELOPMENT

The investment in faculty development almost always proved good
on its return—and then some. Based on the Ford-funded projects, engaging
a faculty member in new scholarship and pedagogy changed more than a
single course; it potentially altered all the courses that faculty member

might teach. Faculty members at campus after campus were universal in their praise of the intellectual awakening that seminar and workshop opportunities triggered. A chorus of voices repeatedly referred to "the different lens" through which they were seeing the world. In many cases, the intellectual changes ran deep indeed. An art professor, for example, said she had become not only a better teacher but also a better artist. She says she now creates different art as a result of her faculty development seminar.

To engage a faculty member also affects more than a single class of students; it potentially influences generations of students. It is also clearly integral to curriculum change. The evaluation highlighted that one cannot improve and rethink the curriculum without offering opportunities for faculty members to rethink what they know. To do that, they need time, experts to turn to, and colleagues locally or nationally with whom to debate responses to the new scholarship that is at once profoundly unsettling and intellectually liberating. Faculty members also need validation from key leadership in their institution, department, or division that investing in such professional development is perceived to be important and valuable.

The designs of faculty development initiatives were richly varied. No single model was necessarily superior, although there were clear trade-offs among models. The institutional culture influenced the model adopted as did the developmental stage of an institution with regard to diversity issues. Everything about the faculty development models varied, beginning with their length. Some institutions like Bemidji chose to do faculty development through a series of four day-long symposia. By contrast, Brandeis designed a five-week summer seminar that met regularly and was very intense. Haverford nested its faculty development model within its regular semester, as did Pitzer, with faculty members meeting once a week for two hours in small groups of eight or less.

For participating in these seminars, most faculty members received either stipends or released time. A few were given stipends for book and photocopying. At Mount St. Mary's, faculty members were given travel money to attend conferences. When the seminar occurred during the semester and the participating faculty member had to attend the seminar as an overload beyond the normal teaching load, it was a serious strain for some faculty members. Institutions chose to organize seminars in a variety of ways. Most had clearly designated leaders who selected the readings and led the discussions. Some, however, like Pitzer and Haverford, each drawing on their egalitarian institutional ethos, opted to run their seminars with no designated leader but rather let the leadership emerge within the seminar itself.

Some institutions preferred to award faculty members individual summer grants to develop a specific course rather than organize a seminar around a set of common readings. Those who opted for this approach enhanced the interchange among faculty members by requiring that they meet with each other two hours a week during their five-week individualized grant period. The faculty at Tulane who were part of such a model insisted that the two-hour weekly meetings were the most valuable aspect of the grant. The opportunity to exchange ideas in the midst of such potentially challenging material seemed a necessity.

Most institutions awarded stipends comparable to what a faculty member might receive teaching a summer course. At Tulane they reduced the original amount slightly so they could award ten faculty grants each summer rather than six because so many faculty members submitted proposals. Bemidji opted for minigrants so they could disperse the money to an even greater number of faculty members in their consortial group.

The composition of a seminar varied nearly as much as its length. Most typically it included only faculty, but many chose to be deliberate about which faculty members they included. Considerations included factors such as departmental representation; level of knowledge of the subject; racial, gender, and ethnic diversity of the participants; variation in faculty rank and age; and what courses they would be revising or creating. Most agreed that frequently the institution's best teachers ended up in these diversity seminars, which was a boon for the project and a gift for the students. The consensus was that it was very important that the seminars have a spectrum of expertise at the table and that some among the group already be grounded in diversity as a scholarly subject matter.

Although most seminars included only faculty, a number of institutions experimented with student involvement in faculty seminars, sometimes attaching students to a faculty member specifically to assist in doing research to redesign a course. In some instances, however, students were full-fledged members of the seminars. Others linked faculty members and administrators, while one included staff. In most instances, the longer the seminar length, the greater the likelihood that the participants were all faculty members.

Establishing a positive climate in the seminar was a key to its success. The faculty at Brandeis spoke of the importance of openness of spirit being the key to its successful five-week intense seminar. You can't, they insisted, have an atmosphere of recrimination. As a Pitzer faculty member put it, without a "suspension of suspicion" it was difficult to create the open-mindedness so critical to dialogue about difference. In the most productive seminars, colleagues were able and willing to learn from one another.

Some of the by-products of the faculty development seminar model were the new opportunities for connections with colleagues. At Brandeis, for instance, it was the first opportunity for part-time, long-term junior faculty to talk to senior faculty. In almost every seminar, it brought people together across disciplines and schools and in some cases linked people with similar but heretofore unknown similar research interests. It was, oddly enough, also a chance to talk to each other as professors about *intellectual* questions instead of internal institutional or departmental politics. It cemented friendships, in some cases, that preceded the seminar but grounded them in intellectual commitments as well as professional ones.

The seminars often were themselves superb training grounds for the exhilarating challenge of teaching diversity courses. One woman said, "I came in with preconceptions of how others think and couldn't have been more mistaken."[8] Her experience echoed some of the peeling away of stereotypes and unexamined perceptions that students in the best diversity courses also reported. In Brandeis' five-week seminar, which more closely parallels the intensity and trust that can be developed over time in a regular course, participants referred to some heart-wrenching moments during which they

For many students, it changed them deeply. "It taught me to speak up about things that bother me and express my identity and feel positive about it"

---

learned a lot from each other because the quality of exchange among the faculty was so remarkable on both an intellectual and an emotional level.

The most useful seminars reminded their participants that it was not enough just to teach subject matter. And even if they wanted to, with diversity as a subject matter it was not always possible. The professor of a course at Haverford College who taught "The Origins of Christian Anti-Semitism" explained that she was not fully prepared for how quickly the interpersonal dynamics and experiential part of the class moved beyond the intellectual. She and the class felt alternately vulnerable and illuminated when the class unleashed such powerful emotions. They all agreed that nonetheless, in the course of the conversations, the students took risks with one another and achieved a level of dialogue that they had not experienced in any other academic setting.

For many students, it changed them deeply. "It taught me to speak up about things that bother me and express my identity and feel positive about it," said one student who had identified herself as having been previously so assimilated that she felt defensive about being a Jew before taking the class. A Christian student said the course "opened me up to the invisibility of Judaism." "This class," said a Jewish student who had felt enormous discomfort purchasing a textbook with a cross on it, "helped me to listen." All of the students looked at their contemporary world with new eyes, which was enhanced by assignments that had them bring in examples from the newspapers and elsewhere of contemporary anti-Semitism to complement their readings on early Christian examples of anti-Semitism. The value of having a diverse classroom was underscored in the different responses to those examples. The Christian students were horrified to discover so much anti-Semitism; by contrast, the Jewish students had come to expect it as part of their daily landscape.[9]

In a number of discussions with students from a variety of Ford-funded institutions, there was a striking contrast between the openness to debate and questions by the faculty teaching the diversity courses and the student peer pressure to conform to a narrower range of views, values, and political positions. It suggests that faculty members and administrators have a crucial role to play in helping students risk certainty and rigid boundaries enough to understand why someone else might have different boundaries. For example, a Hispanic student who described himself as having been a militant Hispanic in an exclusive way, thought only of his own people until he took a course from one of the humanities professors at Brandeis teaching a seminar derived from the Ford faculty development grant. Because of the professor and the course, the student felt challenged to reassess his previous definitive views. Now he is very involved in the student Intercultural Center where students of all colors and classes intermingle and work together on diversity issues.

The Ford Foundation grant had significant power to legitimize the value of faculty members investing time in course development and pedagogical issues. This was especially important at more elite institutions where research was so privileged over teaching. For those at institutions where teaching was more central, these seminars were also important because they provided time and support for faculty members to engage with the scholarly and pedagogical issues of diversity. Most seminars devoted some attention to pedagogical issues, but it was clear this was an under-studied matter. One of the great benefits of diversity was its insistence that professors consider not simply what they teach, but how. Denison's workshop, for instance, had a good balance between concern for the intellectual issues and course content on the one hand, and teaching and learning issues on the other. Similarly, Mount St. Mary's workshops included extensive work on pedagogy.

At Haverford, they very intentionally incorporated pedagogical issues into their weekly discussions, which proved invaluable once they actually had to teach their new Social Justice courses. Some of the pedagogical issues discussed in faculty seminars were cited as being of particular value once they faced students instead of colleagues. Among the most important cited were the role of student sympathies and alliances in determining classroom climate; the extent to which long-cherished or deeply rooted beliefs might or should be challenged by social justice courses; the nature and dangers of stereotyping; the meaning of group membership and its inclusive/exclusive implications; walking the tightrope between the presentation of information (objectivity)

Rooting faculty development in serious
academic and intellectual scholarship has
the most potential for sustaining the
dialogue and fostering engagement

---

and points of view (subjectivity); and maintaining academic integrity in
courses with heavily ideological and personal dimensions.[10]

Those who were part of faculty development seminars, especially
those of longer duration, spoke of the experience as a transformative one intellectually, personally, and pedagogically. Nonetheless, two nagging issues
dogged this approach to institutional diversity. The first was how to multiply
the effect of these seminars beyond the people who participated in them.
Many institutions built in ways to guarantee an impact beyond that of the
seminar. Some required that participants make presentations to their departments, while others organized campus-wide forums, produced videos of seminars and workshops that could be used with other faculty, or created
campus newsletters. In a few instances, however, the influence simply never
traversed beyond those faculty who were direct beneficiaries of the grant.
The second was related to the first: how to overcome the deep-seated resistance some faculty members had to these kinds of efforts. At two campuses,
the resistance among a group of faculty members was so great and so orches-
trated that it distracted many from the intellectual work they wanted to do,
derailed them, or simply wore them out. At another campus, it was not faculty hostility but indifference that limited the impact of the grant.

When Haverford was revamping its original Diversity Requirement
into a Social Justice Requirement, many of the faculty members who supported the new version made the effort to reach out to faculty members who
feared the courses would be ideological indoctrination and lacking in intellectual content. They apparently persuaded skeptical faculty members that indeed these Social Justice courses would be grounded in academic scholarship,
invite a variety of perspectives on an issue, and seek to teach students how to
analyze difficult, highly charged issues. The climate for the subsequent Ford
work was therefore supportive rather than unproductively contentious.

By contrast, at Tulane a series of campus diversity issues had swept
up the community in a whirlwind of controversy that embroiled everyone in
what some referred to as a vitriolic debate that played itself out in polarizing
ways. The situation was exacerbated by the role the media played and the
ties at the local level with a national organization that has a record of in-

flammatory attacks on multiculturalism. Although the waters have calmed and the vocal opposition revealed for the minority position it actually represented among the faculty, there was a heavy price paid for "victory," and an undercurrent of unresolved tensions.

Based on the experience of the Ford-funded projects, there does seem to be the possibility for reduced tension if there is room for sustained dialogue and an attentiveness to the cause of defensiveness by faculty who feel at odds with the diversity policies on campus. To achieve that climate of suspended judgment is difficult, but it is necessary to strive for. Rooting faculty development in serious academic and intellectual scholarship has the most potential for sustaining the dialogue and fostering engagement.

STUDENT-ORIENTED PROJECTS

Although there were fewer instances of projects incorporating students, almost every time students were involved it was a stunning success. The most impressive one occurred at the University of Redlands. If faculty members resisted diversity there, students embraced it with vigor and imagination. And there are surviving, vital structures as testaments to their engagement. Some of the Ford Foundation funds were allocated to students for a multicultural festival. While it is common to hear proponents of multiculturalism deride the food and festival superficiality of some diversity efforts, in point of fact it is often a beginning point, just like the inclusion of a single author, a single issue, a single assignment in a course. In the case of Redlands, the students' festival, called Living on Common Ground, has grown larger and more successful each successive year. Last spring, for example, there was significant involvement of the local community, especially the local high school, in the promotion and implementation of the festival. The event combines ethnic foods, cultural entertainment, and educational programs. The university's student government has taken over the sponsorship of the festival and uses a combination of student fees and university budget support to maintain it.

The Ford Evaluation Team found that
when community service internships were
integrated within courses, they had an
even greater impact

Students have also continued to be a catalyst for change at Redlands with the establishment of an Intercultural Residence Hall and the formation of a sorority and a fraternity organized to look at issues of diversity. It may be the first of its kind in the country. While there may still be some sharp disagreements among faculty members, the mood on campus among the students is punctuated by good will and cooperation. Through their activities, the students have had new opportunities for leadership training and in the process offer models for their peers.

At the University of Iowa two different student groups assumed leadership in Ford-funded diversity initiatives. The teaching assistants who were the moving force in developing a diversity reader for the freshman rhetoric course and those who revised a general education course became an important informal network for each other during and after the work of the grant was completed. Their involvement as graduate students has, of course, significant implications for their careers as professors. Paralleling the graduate students' work, the undergraduate students who were members of Iowa's nationally ranked Forensic Union were funded by Ford to develop topics and resources on race relations and cultural diversity. In this predominantly white school in this predominantly white state—a state with the one of the highest proportions of whites in the nation—their debate team raised diversity issues all across the country and learned the textures of a subject area that they might otherwise not have selected.

Another highly successful model involving students was the minority scholars programs that took different forms but generally involved selecting through a competitive process a group of minority students for research experiences during the summer. All had summer stipends. At Tulane University, six minority students each of two summers were awarded two thousand dollars each for completing a directed research proposal in the area of their intended major. They were required to prepare their proposal and do their research under the guidance of a faculty supervisor. Exceeding all expectations, more than fifty-two students submitted proposals from fifteen different majors over a two-year period.

Several faculty supervisors talked about how the experience transformed them and their understandings about the issues minority students face. One student's summer research project actually led to a new course offering on Asians. Like Tulane's faculty seminar, students in Tulane's minority research program also met as a group during their research summers. For students of color, this was an important source of support for them, which also became a means through which the students developed a deeper attachment to the university. It was also a place where they were affirmed as intellectuals. There was another positive by-product of the minority scholars program at Tulane; because students had to identify professors ahead of time in order to apply, even those who did not get selected found themselves in a newly formed mentoring relationship with faculty members.

Pitzer College's experiment to link students to the local Los Angeles community through internships and volunteer community service was another example of successfully engaging students in diversity issues. What began with ten students volunteering at eleven organizations had leapt by the second year to fifty students volunteering at thirty-three organizations. Short-term volunteer activities seem to be a key to drawing larger number of students. Internships were successful enough to become a permanent part of the career planning function at the college. The Ford Evaluation Team, however, found that when community service internships were integrated within courses, they had an even greater impact.

RESEARCH AND RESOURCE MATERIALS

There were modest awards among the recipients to develop or purchase resources such as new material for the library at Spring Hill and Mount St. Mary's. The diversity reader for the rhetoric course at the University of Iowa was quite ambitious and successful for those who chose to teach from it. Even those who chose not to adopt the text itself seemed more inclined to feel some responsibility to include more diverse texts in their courses because of the existence of the new anthology.

Though the vast majority of the grantees did very little with any kind of technology, the University of Notre Dame did develop, in addition to bibliographic resources for their faculty, some videotapes of portions of their faculty development seminar to be used for future conferences and to orient new faculty members.

The standout for originality and ambition and ultimately for stunning success in the category of new research technology was without question the Black History Archives Project at Virginia Commonwealth University. It began as an attempt to create a body of historical research documents about the life of black people in the Richmond area. The first major challenge of the project was to create trust and cooperation with the black community with which VCU had a rather sketchy history of collaboration until recently. Both new presidential leadership and the impact over time of the archives program locally led ultimately to a new awareness of interdependency between VCU and the Richmond community. "VCU is inseparable from the urban environment in which it resides," read a new strategic plan. It continued, "Extensive interaction with the Richmond metropolitan region yields a two-way flow of benefits between the University and the community, and generates capabilities for addressing urban issues throughout the nation and the world."[11] The second major challenge was to develop an archives collection that could be tied to the new computer technologies and ultimately linked to students doing research in specific courses.

By the end of the project, the connections with the community had been forged to such an extent that they were ready to reach out beyond the Richmond community to Norfolk. They also intend eventually to connect the archives to the world at large through the Internet. In hopes they might persuade other communities to contribute archival materials, they have also developed a video that describes the archives project in some detail.

4 Institutionalizing Project Goals and Planning Next Steps: Small Steps and Bold Visions

> The conditions of truth and the conditions of democracy are one and the same: as there is freedom, as the community is open and inclusive and the exchange of ideas thorough and spirited, so there is both more democracy and more learning, more freedom and more knowledge (which becomes, here, ideas conditionally agreed upon)....Learning communities, like all free communities, function only when their members conceive of themselves as empowered to participate fully in the common activities that define the community—in this case, learning and the pursuit of knowledge in the name of common living.[12]
>
> Benjamin Barber, *Education for Democracy*

One of the central concerns for both the grantee and the funder is what impact the project had on the institution as a whole. A second concern is how to sustain the momentum for reform once the external money evaporates. It is an especially vexing problem in this time of financial constrictions in higher education. Although too often the funder underestimates the serious limitations of institutional resources and overestimates the capacities of a college to perpetuate a grant-funded project, grant recipients could exercise more imagination and intentionality about how to institutionalize at least some pieces of formerly grant-funded projects. In the Ford Foundation proposals, like so many others, the application required that each institution show evidence that it would continue the work of the grant in an appropriate way after there were no longer external funds from the Ford Foundation. Routinely applicants promise to continue the work of the grant either without seriously thinking through their obligations or knowing full well that the escape clause rested in the phrase, "as appropriate."

It is self-defeating to put out a traditional job
description with no mention of expertise in the
scholarship of diversity and then, after the fact,
be disappointed that one cannot find someone
who can also teach diversity courses

Lip service is a dangerous thing, however, and many a superb project withers after grant money is depleted. It is neither desirable, necessary, nor even particularly responsible to simply pack up one's tent and utensils once the grant is over and go back to life as before. Among the Ford grantees there was ample evidence of some of the many possible ways to extend the life of the grant by institutionalizing aspects of it. Below are examples of strategies adopted by some of the nineteen Ford-funded projects, mixed with a few that they did not adopt but should perhaps have considered.

INSTITUTIONALIZING DIVERSITY INITIATIVES

Diversity requirements. Timing is everything here. At some institutions like Wesleyan University, a diversity requirement is not the preferred curricular strategy for assuring diversity. At others, the blood on the floor and scars on the skin are simply not worth the bitter skirmish to achieve a diversity requirement. But in many colleges, such as Haverford College, the University of Iowa, Denison University, and Mount St. Mary's with its six-unit requirement for all students, a diversity requirement guarantees that newly developed diversity courses have a more permanent home in the curriculum.

New staff lines. This is a way to guarantee that there is someone in charge of making sure the goals of the project have a life after the grant. Pitzer created a permanent position for a community internship coordinator and Redlands created a new student life position that had a focus on cultural diversity programming. Spring Hill appointed a director of their new Multicultural Office and one colleague remarked, "It was unexpected that even at a small college like Spring Hill one person and the creation of a one-person office could have such a transforming impact."[13]

New faculty lines. As a routine mechanism for ensuring that diversity is institutionalized, departments should consider writing job descriptions that include diversity as a central or partial part of the job requirement. It is self-defeating to put out a traditional job description with no mention of expertise in the scholarship of diversity and then, after the fact, be disappointed that one cannot find someone who can also teach diversity courses.

When altering a job description isn't sufficient, sometimes an entirely new faculty line is called for. Redlands, for example, created a new faculty position in Race and Ethnicity. Then, when the highly skilled person in diversity leaves, the expertise is retained in the job line even if the personnel shift.

Course descriptions. Like job descriptions, course descriptions that include diversity in them contribute to a more permanent likelihood of institutional transformation. They also ensure that diversity is dependent not on some individualized preference on the part of a particular instructor but rather on the responsible coverage required of any professor who might teach the course.

New academic programs. In some programs, a project leads logically to a new program, which is, of course, another way to institutionalize the project. At Tulane, for instance, they are developing a Cultural Studies Program that was in formation before the Ford grant but that has emerged more quickly as a result of the kind of faculty research generated by the diversity seminars. Sometimes diversity projects lead to the formation of women's studies, ethnic studies, or gay and lesbian studies programs, which also can offer a structure for sustaining already developed courses and for instigating new ones later on. The Ford project, for instance, at Boston College contributed toward the movement to develop an Asian American Studies Program.

New structures with diversity as a central focus. Many campuses are discovering that they need some sort of structure to coordinate all the many diversity activities on their campuses. In some cases, without such a coordinating structure the synergy is missing that gives coherence to otherwise disparate and individually weaker units. Notre Dame has created a presidential committee on cultural diversity that is to be chaired by the executive assistant to the president. Among other things, it plans to do a diversity assessment of departments. The English department at the University of Iowa took the initiative at the departmental level by creating its own departmental diversity task force. Brandeis established a faculty diversity committee to assist departments in their search for diverse faculty members.

A member of the committee participates in every faculty search process and signs off on it at the end. Brandeis also established a new Intercultural Center for students that is now located in an attractive new space. Another institution has a Faculty Colloquium on Cultural Diversity, which now is an ongoing site for diversity outreach and education.

Adding a new diversity component to an already existing structure. Even more expedient than creating entirely new structures is embedding a diversity component within a current structure on campus. At Boston College, an existing faculty social justice group, Xocomil, that originally focused only on human rights in Latin America eventually evolved in collaboration with the Ford project to become the conduit through which information on cultural diversity of all kinds reaches the faculty. A Teaching and Learning Center is a perfect example of a structure that is set up to do the kind of dissemination work and carry on the expertise generated by many projects. A once externally funded set of faculty development grants can also become a specially designated part of the yearly allocated monies for more general summer grants to faculty members. Again, writing a diversity component into the mission or responsibility of the existing structure is preferable.

Development of permanent resources. Projects like Iowa's diversity reader for the first-year rhetoric course or the materials developed for their forensic union remain a potent influence after the grant itself is completed. So do audiovisual and new library resources or innovative projects like the Black History Archives Project at Virginia Commonwealth University and the computer program developed at Wesleyan University to map diversity courses. Mount St. Mary's College has produced monographs and videos as well as faculty and student materials, which are housed in the library as a resource for the whole campus. The involvement of their campus librarian at all stages of the project helped ensure ongoing development and dissemination of resources.

Cultivation of other sources of funding for diversity initiatives. The common wisdom is that money begets money. A Ford Foundation grant should, in able hands, make it easier to raise additional money for other projects. Sometimes these projects are really continuations of the first one.

At Tulane, for example, the Ford funds for the minority scholars program were replaced by funds from Coca-Cola after the Ford grant expired. Haverford turned from Ford to the Philip Morris Foundation that funded not a faculty development project as Ford had done but a student leadership project, which was a logical next step after the Ford grant. At Tulane, the Newcomb College Foundation offers its own stipends to faculty members doing new courses on women and has become one source of continued funding for projects previously funded by Ford.

Making permanent what was a grant-funded cultural activity. For grants that produced cultural events, it may be possible to shelter them within an existing structure, or, like Redlands, make them a new part of the academic landscape. The student-run spring festival that has grown so much larger and involved significant portions of the townspeople is now entirely run by the student government, which receives its funding from student activity fees.

Mechanisms for multiplying the effects of a faculty development seminar. Just because the formal funding for a faculty development seminar has ended does not mean that the exchanges and outreach to other faculty members cannot take place. In some cases, faculty members need to empower themselves and simply take charge and make sure this is done. There was a surprising passivity in several faculty groups that had been inspired by their experience but once the grant was over felt reluctant to assume authority for figuring out how to disseminate what they learned to some of their colleagues. Faculty members could set up special campuswide presentations together, or each could go back to their department and arrange for a workshop or a presentation. Not every workshop comes with a stipend. On their own initiative or with the cooperation of an administrator, faculty members could organize a half-day workshop or offer to run the all-day faculty workshop or retreat that is a regularly scheduled part of the calendar. Doing a guest lecture in a colleague's class is another way to multiply the effects of a grant as is team-teaching with a colleague who wasn't in the grant but wanted to be.

If diversity can begin to be a pre-thought
instead of an afterthought, it would
have a more immediate impact on
institutional culture

Building diversity into strategic planning. If diversity can begin to
be a pre-thought instead of an afterthought, it would have a more immediate
impact on institutional culture. This is an approach to institutionalizing diversity that is especially effective when one has strong leadership from top
administrators, the very people who do most of the strategic planning on
campuses. Once it is interjected from the beginning, diversity can affect
everything from recruitment to retention to residence halls to hiring faculty
to sexual harassment policy to parental leaves and partner benefits. The most
powerful element enters when an institution frames its mission as educating
all students to live in a pluralistic society. From this mission, effective dialogues can take place and serious structural reform be implemented. Mount
St. Mary's College, for example, clearly has had such leadership from its
board and senior administrators as it created its strategic institutional plan,
which has, in turn, garnered the school national visibility for its efforts.

Vision. The "vision thing" doesn't sound like it is a vehicle for making diversity permanent, but it is crucial to its endurance. "Without vision,
the people will perish" says the proverb. Having a long-range vision of where
you want to go and what kind of academic community you are striving to
create can ensure that diversity is melded with the mission of the college.
Both Pitzer and Mount St. Mary's, for instance, place diversity at the center
of their vision for the college, a factor that has facilitated the important work
they have done in this area both locally and nationally. Paired with vision is
the clear sense of concrete steps that need to be taken to get there, a sense of
sequencing and interrelatedness. As the vice president for academic affairs at
Redlands put it, "While we still have a long way to go to create the fully
aware intercultural academic community envisioned in our grant, we believe
the short-term objectives have been substantially achieved and have provided impetus and momentum for continuing on the longer journey."[14]

NETWORKING

Another strategy for institutionalizing diversity and multiplying its
effects rests in networking. The greater the number of people involved, the

greater the likelihood that diversity will not melt away. Networks come in all sizes, places, and now with our technological advances, they come with all sorts of unpronounceable names and addresses. Below are some suggested networking ideas.

Internal networks. Networks need not be fancy or well funded. They also need not be formal. Some of the most effective networks are the informal ones that evolve from an externally funded project. Several of the Ford-funded projects spawned just these kinds of informal networks. Many grew out of faculty development seminars where a group cohesiveness continued after the seminar was over. The seminar as the principal cause of connection has been superceded by colleagueship, newfound common research interests, a team-teaching project, a collaborative research venture, a discussion of pedagogy. Some seminar participants even choose to continue to meet as a group on a regular monthly basis. The graduate students at Iowa have formed a study group as a follow-up to their work together on the Ford project. At Spring Hill College, a rather remarkable network evolved out of diversity work done on campus that eventually led to a collaborative enterprise outside the campus when professional staff and maintenance staff worked together at some local Baptist churches. Student networks from minority scholars programs and cultural diversity groups emerged, some of which were formalized like the Intercultural Center at Brandeis or the sorority and fraternity at Redlands that are to be organized around examining diversity issues. One of the most valuable offshoots of networking, formal or informal, is the continuous communication that it helps to foster, a communication that is critical to sustaining diversity initiatives.

External networks. There are a number of options for external networks. Most are pre-existing ones that are not likely to include diversity unless you insist on its inclusion, which some networks are perfectly happy to accommodate. For example, Denison University is a member of a consortium called the Great Lakes Colleges Association (GLCA). While diversity was not the purpose that drew this regional network of twelve colleges together, GLCA has included diversity as a focus of many of its meetings and workshops. The Ford Foundation awarded a grant to GLCA to support their

One of the most stunning surprises for the Ford Evaluation Team was how little assessment was done....it is imperative that the next generation of diversity projects incorporate ways to map progress and flag problems by integrating assessment into projects from the very beginning

---

plan to offer summer workshops on multiculturalism. GLCA then turned to a Denison University faculty member who had benefitted from the Ford grant on his own campus to teach one of their new summer workshops. The networks thus become mutually beneficial to all concerned.

In some geographic areas, a group might need to invent a regional diversity center where there isn't one. Many schools that are themselves not particularly diverse racially are seeking special partnerships with historically black colleges and universities. Tulane University has such a partnership with Xavier University of Louisiana. There could also be more outreach for partnership with Hispanic-serving institutions, tribal colleges, and women's colleges. Bemidji's Ford project linked it with Arrowhead Community College System, which serves many Native Americans, and in their interaction as a consortium, they wisely changed locations for the various symposia, having one of them on one of the several Indian reservations in the county.

What began as a computer networking project to categorize all the diversity courses at Wesleyan University has had two interesting networking by-products: one internal, the other external. Although Wesleyan had prided itself on the number of diversity courses generated across the curriculum, students found it difficult to map their way to a coherent intellectual program of study because the offerings were so widely dispersed. Through the Ford-funded diversity computer program, students discovered how to select a complementary set of courses that satisfied their desire for coherence. Several departments at Wesleyan were so impressed that they asked those who had mapped diversity courses to map various fields of study within departmental offerings. In doing so, departments took a fresh look at their curriculum and redesigned courses accordingly. Wesleyan University has begun to map the entire curriculum. The designers of the Wesleyan computer mapping project have taken their model to several national and regional organizations that have themselves already initiated their own diversity projects. Through a national editorial board, the groups are in the process of creating *Diversity Connections*, an interactive computer program for faculty and staff members, students, and administrators around the country who want to investigate the range of curricular and institutional diversity work occurring nationwide.

Networks with the local community. Despite the fact many academic institutions often have an uneasy relationship with their local community, when the networks are established, it is a splendid way of sustaining diversity initiatives. Community service projects frequently open the door to such collaborations, as evident in the Pitzer College project, but so do research and technical assistance projects like some developed at Tulane University. Projects like the Black History Archives Project at Virginia Commonwealth University are a natural way to forge solid networks with the community.

Electronic networks. We are just beginning to understand some of the ways the electronic networks will transform our capacities to communicate with one another. Virginia Commonwealth plans to experiment with it to make their model available to a broader audience. Wesleyan University's computer mapping project for diversity has expanded to the campus as a whole and soon will, in another form, be part of a national network of people working on diversity issues. The Association of American Colleges and Universities, a recipient of a Ford diversity grant after these initial nineteen institutions received theirs, has already set up Diverse, an electronic, interactive bulletin board so that several hundred faculty members in its Curriculum and Faculty Development Diversity Network can talk to one another. AAC&U's electronic network has also opened its electronic, interactive bulletin board to other Ford Foundation and Lilly Endowment grantees working on diversifying the curriculum.

ASSESSMENT

One of the most stunning surprises for the Ford Evaluation Team was how little assessment was done. Anywhere. In any form. Except in the most perfunctory ways, it was largely ignored as the valuable resource it can be for illuminating issues and improving learning. Thus far, in campus diversity work, assessment is woefully underdeveloped. The team believes it is imperative that the next generation of diversity projects incorporate ways to map progress and flag problems by integrating assessment into projects from the very beginning.

The team saw little evidence that projects followed such a path. By the end of its grant, however, Mount St. Mary's had begun to develop tools for institutional assessment along with student outcomes assessment. There are numerous ways any institution might have begun to gather data even if, at the outset, it focused on only one or two particularly important questions to the project. For example, does this new diversity course alter the way students respond to people different than they are? What is the intellectual journey faculty members traverse in faculty development seminars that makes them receptive to the new scholarship on diversity? How has the summer student research program for minority students affected their sense of themselves as students, their later academic achievement, or their plans for graduate school? What has the effect been on campus race relations of student-led cultural events about diversity?

Some of this data might have been readily available in routine assignments: papers, exams, journals, group presentations. Others might have been collected from exit interviews, focus groups, or a specially designed questionnaire asking students or faculty to assess personal changes. In some of the Ford projects, needed information was scattered and uncoordinated. No dean kept track of the academic careers of students in minority summer research projects; departments didn't either. No project seemed to monitor how a faculty development seminar affected the kinds of courses participating faculty members beyond the one course earmarked for the grant, although Brandeis' and Pitzer's self-reports from faculty members about the impact of the project on their work and on themselves illustrate how powerful such tools can be in evaluating the overall long-range impact of faculty development. To secure the most useful data will, in many cases, require the coordination of several institutional areas—two or three departments, a dean's office, a career office—and the coordination will need to continue over time. How many students, for example, who were part of a minority scholars research summer project continued in their major, went on to graduate or medical school, and became scientists or faculty members?

With such data, involved faculty members and staff can more effectively demonstrate the educational value of the project to their colleagues and thus begin to expand the base of support. Most importantly, the project itself can be improved as it learns what works, what doesn't, and why. New assessment questions can be asked each year to enlarge knowledge about learning, about institutional change, and about building more cohesive and mutually committed communities.

There are many assessment models that have emerged in the last decade that are user-friendly, faculty-staff-and-student driven, qualitative as well as quantitative, and free of irrelevant, perfunctory but time-consuming externally produced questionnaires. Assessment is now a tool available to all of us, even those of us without extensive expertise in variables, statistical analyses, and computer programming. There is no need to wait for external experts. We can begin to define problem areas, specific issues of concern on a particular campus, and critical questions at the local level. Monitoring institutional change is serious business—and it can be a source of future planning, useful information, and new visions for the future.

In creating an assessment design, we need to be very aware of through whose lens we are studying diversity. In fact, multiple perspectives—usually three on a single question—have proved to be the most illuminating, balanced, and accurate. If, for example, we are asking about institutional change, there may be a number of valid, if conflicting, perspectives. From a president or vice president we may hear about the progress—changes in the percentage of students of color, for example. From a staff member of color we may be invited to see a very different perspective. We may see job descriptions that look no different, hiring/retention decisions that result in no new faculty members or not retaining others, all done with sincere explanations. Or we may see budget cuts hitting some areas more than others. Students involved in coordinating a cultural event or voluntary community service project may be differently affected by diversity issues than students not involved. Students of color involved in such a project may have a different assessment of its overall impact than white students.

The commitment to diversity is a challenging one. It continually reshapes our questions, our definitions, and our visions. On many campuses it appears that the real work begins when there is sufficient diversity of per-

The commitment to diversity is a challenging one. It continually reshapes our questions, our definitions, and our visions

spectives to begin the dialogue. It is, however, at such a moment that inevitably some of the greatest tensions emerge. Although assessing individual projects on diversity needs to be fully integrated into proposals, it is also important to monitor institutional progress as a whole. On the assumption that this will be a long and intense process, the Evaluation Team offers the following set of questions as one way to assess the degree of institutionalization and resources available to the institution.

1. Because faculty development efforts are largely volunteer, to what degree have revised courses or infusion efforts continued after a particular faculty member has left? Are hiring and job descriptions different as a result, or is expertise in issues related to diversity still viewed as a "nice addition?"

2. Does the project require the sustained efforts and talents of a single person or a few people who might well burn out if their services are required at the level now being asked, or is there a growing set of internal resources? The question is, "Can this wonderful project or effort be sustained?"

3. Is the job of raising issues, bringing up questions, providing expertise shared among increasing numbers of people, or a small few?

4. Has there been sustainable commitment and are there resources at all levels after the external funding has been depleted?

5. To what degree has there been a synergy among efforts—a process by which the impact of any one effort has been seen as connected to the efforts of others? Or have many discrete activities each operated on its own—serving to add to a list of diversity activities but not serving to build an impact greater than the parts? To what degree, for example, have student affairs and academic affairs complemented one another?

6. Has there been institutionalized reflection, dialogue, and information about where the institution is, from where has it come, and what are its next steps?

7. Is it clear where such dialogues should take place, and is there widespread feeling that multiple perspectives on issues of progress, next steps, strengths, and weaknesses will be incorporated?

8. Is the rhetoric of institutional commitment in place? At the same time, is there a perception from those most critically involved that the institution "walk the talk," as several people have described it?

For many years, we talked about the challenge of diversity, the problems of diversity, with an implication that increasing attention to diversity brought with it problems. It has become clear that as we engage issues of diversity, we uncover the vulnerable and dysfunctional elements in our institutions and communities. Things that we once could ignore, we no longer can accept as a given—whether it be ineffectiveness in traditional teaching and learning, weaknesses in faculty advising, absence of community, separation of student and academic affairs, an overemphasis on publishing, rigid hiring practices, departmental fiefdoms, harassment, and discrimination, just to name a few. We now have an opportunity to assess and engage these issues in the urgent context of diversity and perhaps to address them in ways we never before thought possible. Our challenge will be to develop assessment approaches that capture the story of our institutions without either bureaucratizing or romanticizing them.

5 Lessons Learned, or I Wish I Had Thought of This Before I Started

[The faculty development] institute was good at helping us develop a strong sense of our own identities and [teaching us] how to talk across our differences to find commonalities. It makes us optimistic that this small mode of democracy and diversity can be achieved on a broader, institutional scale.[15]

a faculty member

From its inception, the design of this evaluation report sought to tease out lessons from the nineteen specific Ford-funded campus projects that might be of immediate and more general use to other campuses at the threshold of implementing diversity initiatives. As each Evaluation Team member made site visits, she structured her evaluation to highlight what people had learned in the process of completing their grant. When the team came together as a group, we tested the results from our particular campuses to see whether a common pattern of insights had emerged from campus representatives who had been interviewed and from our own assessments as evaluators. We looked in particular for lessons learned in hindsight that might be more generally applied in a variety of campus settings. The groups below, therefore, represent both the accumulated wisdom of participants from the nineteen Ford-funded institutions and the collective expertise of the four authors of this report, who have been evaluating diversity initiatives in a broad range of campus environments over the past decade.

The team has singled out seven major areas of concern in initiating and implementing diversity projects.

1. Building consensus and considering context
2. Maximizing the impact of the grant
3. Structuring the grant
4. Engaging faculty

Building a broad consensus and drawing
upon already existing leadership from a
representative constituency works better
than mandates imposed from above without
previous dialogue and support

---

5. Rethinking the curriculum

6. Securing financial and administrative support

7. Involving student affairs in diversity efforts

Under each heading, we have clustered suggestions in almost a checklist format. All of these seven areas are critical components of strategic thinking that an institution should engage in with the larger campus community when undertaking major diversity initiatives. The four evaluators have opted to frame our final overview as a series of lessons learned in hopes that future efforts at institutional reform might be smoother, more sustained, and have greater overall impact.

BUILDING CONSENSUS AND CONSIDERING CONTEXT

- The strongest projects involved constituents from a wide variety of groups on campus in the planning, implementation, and follow-up stages. For some this meant reaching out to a broad spectrum of faculty leaders from the senate to influential faculty member to faculty members from a range of departments. No one involved the board of trustees, but several realized afterwards that such a strategy would have been wise. A number of grant recipients engaged students in all three stages of the grant with predictably beneficial results to all concerned.

- It is a tautology, but projects that don't reach out beyond a small core of committed people typically don't reach more than a small group of committed people.

- Some of the strongest diversity projects were undertaken after extensive debate and dialogue within the college at large; and if consensus can be reached on overall commitments and strategies, the chances for a productive project are greatly enhanced.

- As valuable as strong leadership from top administrators is, it is not enough in and of itself to sustain a sound diversity plan. Building a broad consensus and drawing upon already existing leadership from a representative constituency works better than mandates imposed from above without previous dialogue and support. However, strong leadership from the top in concert with a broad base of support maximizes the momentum, the clarity, and the academic community's full commitment.

- In consortial projects, it is important that leadership of project activities is shared among participating institutions so that valuable resources and potential leadership are expanded. Also in consortial projects, the decision making for a project needs to be shared in order to build reciprocal, solid relationships among the various constituents in the group.

- It is important not to underestimate the significance of public relations, publicity, public understanding, and local institutional support; this is a way to educate the campus, the local community, alumni and parents, and the broader public. It can eliminate some of the misinformation that can polarize a campus, and it can buoy the spirits and lengthen the commitment of those who labor hard at what, too often, is unrecognized and unrewarded work.

MAXIMIZING THE IMPACT OF THE GRANT

- Most diversity projects flourish when they are built upon preceding efforts to diversify the campus. There is a direct correlation between the success of a grant and the institution's history of commitment to diversity. When there is a history and a mission, a climate of support and a commitment, a consensus and receptivity to the idea of curricular and pedagogical transformation, projects thrive. If there has been significant campus discussion and a degree of consensus about diversity on campus before a diversity project is initiated, it accelerates and smooths the process enormously.

- Diversity has opened up unforeseen opportunities for collaboration across groups that otherwise might remain aloof from one another. Evidence of this is apparent in collaborations between universities and community colleges, students and faculty members, academic and student affairs, and people from the local community and those within academia itself.

Without diversity in the project personnel, the impact of the grant will be more limited

- Projects enhance their likelihood of success when they build upon an institution's existing strengths and use them as the vehicle for launching diversity initiatives.

- Timing isn't everything, but it's a lot. Some of the most successful projects tied themselves to or were the unintended beneficiaries of other major events or decisions on campus. For example, one grant was awarded to a college whose faculty had just endorsed a social justice requirement in its curriculum; another was awarded a grant just before the College of Liberal Arts passed a general education diversity requirement.

- Since creating a genuinely diverse academic institution is not a short-time fix but something that can only be achieved over time with serious commitment and focus, projects needed to find ways to sustain themselves or continue progress on their goals after the grant money ends. Thinking through structures that might institutionalize the goals of the grant is critical. Working with administrators to achieve such long-term goals is a must.

STRUCTURING THE GRANT

- Without diversity in the project personnel, the impact of the grant will be more limited.

- Single remedies or single solutions for what are complex, intertwined issues will fail to address the long-term institutional issues concerning diversity.

- Authoritarian leadership usually hampers the long-term effectiveness of a diversity project, while shared leadership that strives to engender a sense of wider ownership typically extends the overall impact of a project.

- Scattered, diffused, and autonomous diversity efforts are less effective than well-coordinated initiatives that are seen as part of a larger institutional effort and thus harness energy for the work to be done.

- Any time new technology is part of a diversity project, one needs to allow for additional lead time so it can be fully integrated into the rest of the project.

- The most carefully structured grants can't always anticipate unforeseen events: the failure of an anticipated diversity curricular change to be approved by the faculty, the success of a curricular change that as a result eliminates a former diversity component, a major governance restructuring that distracts everyone from diversity initiatives, a financial crisis that redirects institutional concerns. In the face of such events, flexibility, inventiveness, and keeping one's sights on the big picture are essential.

- Without an assessment component, a project can't know what is worth replicating elsewhere on campus; without assessment a project denies itself a valuable means of persuading others of the project's value; without assessment, flawed programming is continued unknowingly; without assessment, it is difficult to plan logical next steps.

ENGAGING FACULTY

- It is always important to have multiple entry points for faculty members to engage with the intellectual and social questions raised by diversity. Some with little knowledge, for instance, may benefit from a more broad-based introductory workshop, while those with more expertise may be more willing to commit to a more intensive seminar. Some may respond more positively to discipline-focused lectures and workshops, others to pedagogical issues.

- The most successful faculty initiatives avoided polarizing faculty opinions and sought creative, varied ways to generate dialogue in an atmosphere of genuine inquiry and mutual respect. The long-term success of a diversity project is often measured by the multiplier effect: how many other faculty members eventually joined in the curricular reform efforts?

- Investment in faculty development is typically a sound one. There are a wide range of models for faculty development ranging from more expensive, time-intensive collaborative summer seminars to structured weekly meetings during the semester involving a small group of faculty members to stipends awarded to individual faculty member to work largely alone to create new courses. While each model has different strengths and weaknesses, the usual by-products include reinvigorating faculty members, producing new courses, bringing new attention to teaching and learning, and spawning new faculty colleagueship that eventually supports future diversity activities.

- The most successful faculty development efforts have focused on the intellectual core of the new scholarship on diversity. This allows faculty members to benefit professionally from their investment in curricular reform, motivates them to continue their work after the seminar is over, and keeps faculty members involved in ways that are consistent with faculty culture and are therefore likely to endure. These efforts also give a legitimacy to diversity which focusing only on the changing demographics of students does not. Moreover, it broadens the number of faculty members who can and will participate.

- The autonomy of the faculty can be a hindrance to a diversity project by creating pockets of unevenness throughout departments, points of resistance that limit the scope of the project, and proprietary course turf wars that undermine genuine curriculum reform. The challenge is to persuade faculty of the intellectual merit of the diversity initiatives and make the challenge professionally irresistible.

- One needs to recognize that not everyone will be eager to participate. Nevertheless, creating an exciting and participatory approach will tend to attract those who are open to new issues.

- It is important to think strategically about which faculty members to encourage to participate in faculty development projects. This is especially the case in curricular reform efforts where there might be a high turnover of faculty, such as general education courses taught by a rotating group of graduate students or part-time instructors. In the midst of such flux, efforts may not be sustained without continued faculty development initiatives structured into the teaching expectations.

• To invest money in training a faculty member to teach a new course, and then not provide a way for him or her to be relieved from other departmental courses to teach it is not a wise use of funds. To fund faculty members to team-teach interdisciplinary courses during a grant and then to cease to fund them to do it after the grant is over is also not a wise use of funds or faculty time.

RETHINKING THE CURRICULUM

• Although not every school can create women's studies or ethnic studies programs, such programs typically provide an institutionalized source of continuing expertise and attentiveness to issues of race, class, gender, and sexual orientation and usually an attentiveness to pedagogical issues as well. Having ethnic studies and women's studies faculty is not sufficient in and of itself to diversify a campus. Nonetheless, it may facilitate diversifying the faculty, diversifying the curriculum, and providing internal resources for continuing efforts.

• When addressing diversity issues that will predictably stir strong emotional responses in students, creating smaller classes is of great importance. Some of those classes may simply be in the original size of the course, others may be in smaller group discussions set up on a regular basis within a larger lecture course. However, small size becomes crucial if one is trying to hammer out differences, build trust, create an atmosphere where one might feel comfortable disclosing some more personal issues, and where exchange is essential.

• Campuses that focus on the intellectual issues tend to have an impact in departments and disciplines as well as in general education. Those who see the issue solely in terms of giving students *some* information tend to

Whatever the diversity project, its success was
enhanced by three elements: it was voluntary, it
had administrative support, and there were stipends
available, which validated the importance of the
project and of faculty, student, or staff time

focus attention on general education alone. To revise general education
without having a long-term plan for revising other aspects of the curriculum is shortsighted.

- Since diversity courses involve not only the subject matter itself, but also
a response to that subject matter, to ignore pedagogical issues is to limit
the effectiveness of the courses.

- With diversity questions as with other intellectual issues, students need a
series of structured curricular opportunities that are sequenced with a developmental model in mind. As students become more sophisticated
about diversity questions, it is important to create new ways that courses
and assignments can challenge and stretch them over time. Diversity
therefore needs to permeate the curriculum both laterally (in several
freshman courses) and vertically (in courses students take sequentially).

- Opening the boundaries between the college and the surrounding communities is an important way to hone a deeper, more accurate understanding of diversity. Such relationships of respectful reciprocity are essential if
progress is to be made in how we live, learn, and work together. Voluntary
internships and community service may be even more transformative
when they are connected to courses and majors.

SECURING FINANCIAL AND ADMINISTRATIVE SUPPORT

- Whatever the diversity project, its success was enhanced by three elements: it was voluntary, it had administrative support, and there were
stipends available, which validated the importance of the project and of
faculty, student, or staff time.

- There is little substitute for strong administrative support for diversity efforts. Presidential leadership and the leadership of key administrative people often determine the centrality or marginality of a project and often determine if the grass-roots supporters simply burn out faster. Such administrative leaders can also influence whether a grant is institutionalized once the external funding has evaporated.

- Awarding minigrants can provide the opportunity for many kinds of faculty and students to get involved in a diversity project. Minigrants take away the fear of writing full-fledged grants and are easier for most people to write. Having once written a minigrant, those new to the area of proposal writing become less intimidated about writing longer grants.

- As institutions broaden their mission statements to include diversity as a central educational goal, the role of the board of trustees can be very important. They can provide support to campus leadership, influence local and national communities of opinion, and offer an overarching vision for their institution. In beginning to engage in such work, boards should also assess their own part of the house. That is, they should examine the composition of their own board membership. It came as a shock to the Evaluation Team that among Ford Foundation diversity grant recipients there was frequently very little racial, gender, and age diversity on boards of trustees at institutions where the rest of the campus was working hard to grapple with diversity issues and in many cases to diversify the composition of the institution. Boards should be out front, not lagging behind the reform initiatives and practices of the institutions over which they have primary oversight.

INVOLVING STUDENT AFFAIRS IN DIVERSITY EFFORTS

- Links between student affairs and academic affairs need to be strengthened if stretched resources and expertise are to be maximized and if the entire campus is to be involved. As one student affairs person put it on her campus, "We are ahead of the faculty in diversity issues because we see firsthand the hurtful obstacles students endure as they get their education."[16] Since students live most of their lives outside of the classroom, curricular projects that ignore ties with student affairs limit the impact and duration of their projects. Instead of piecemeal, uncoordinated efforts,

Whatever faculty members or administrators do about diversity, most students are living out the issues of diversity daily, personally, in a sometimes confused way, often with great pain, sometimes with eloquence and creativity

academic and student affairs should foster the kind of routine interconnections in their work that might illuminate the complex dynamic of students' intellectual and personal development. Such fruitful reciprocity between both sides of the house would create new knowledge, which is currently stymied by the present arrangement of separate and unequal institutional divisions.

- Students see and experience the world in dramatically different ways than faculty members or administrators. Whatever faculty members or administrators do about diversity, most students are living out the issues of diversity daily, personally, in a sometimes confused way, often with great pain, sometimes with eloquence and creativity.

- It is extremely important that campuses have a variety of forums and arenas where students can carry on their developmental issues related to diversity beyond the classroom. It matters, for example, that Jewish students have Hillel or that students of color have a multicultural center or that women have a women's center.

6 Implications for the Next Generation of Diversity Projects

> As Americans, we originally came from many different shores, and our diversity has been at the center of the making of America. While our stories contain the memories of different communities, together they inscribe a larger narrative. Filled with what Walt Whitman celebrated as the "varied carols" of America, our history generously gives all of us our "mystic chords of memory."...Our denied history "bursts with telling."[17]
> Ronald Takaki, *A Different Mirror: A History of Multicultural America*

The experiences of nineteen colleges and universities who sought to enhance understandings about diversity through Ford-funded projects offer insights into how we might proceed with the next generation of efforts at building more inclusive communities and improving the quality of education by making diversity a central educational goal. The most important of those insights is that creating genuinely inclusive academic institutions is not a quick fix but a long-term commitment. It is a commitment that can certainly build upon the past, but it also requires vision and risk since we will be inventing a state of affairs that has yet to be achieved and is not yet even fully imagined. Many academics who talk about a commitment to diversity don't always recognize the extent to which the entire university or college will need to change in order to achieve genuine equity and inclusion. How one assesses progress toward that goal often depends on how close one is to the center or norm around which the institution has organized itself over its history.

There was, for example, on a number of campuses the Evaluation Team visited, a dissonance between what minority faculty and staff members mean by diversity and transformation, and what white faculty and staff

The best practices recognized the inaccuracy of reducing a person to a single, narrowly construed identity. They avoided simplistic notions that any of us carry a single identity that should determine what one studies, whom one teaches, or which group one counsels

members mean by diversity. Minority faculty and staff members see diversity as more transformative than their white colleagues. They expect concrete changes in the way the institution responds to their presence, in policies, practice, programs, and curriculum. White administrators, faculty members, and students often see diversity as enhancing what is already there, rather than rethinking what they do. Because we don't always realize that we hold dramatically different perceptions, we are sometimes surprised when one group is so discontent while another is basking in the glow of accomplishment.

On most of the nineteen campuses, *diversity* remained an elusive term. One of its great strengths is the elasticity of the term. Its value resides in the fact that as our understandings about differences expand to embrace more categories, the word *diversity* can still be used. In most cases, however, institutions—quite logically—begin with the diversity found in the constituents currently served. To end with only an understanding of immediate demographic diversities is, however, to ignore the enormous body of scholarship about difference, to ill-prepare students for the wider diversity they are likely to encounter in their lives, and to miss an opportunity to wrestle with the greater complexities of national and global diversity. It would also falsely suggest that the many states where racial diversity might be limited need not concern themselves with the histories, cultures, and experiences of non-white racial minorities.

An exciting breakthrough emerged at the University of Iowa, a predominantly white institution, in which the diversity project made it very clear that diversity initiatives were not just for students of color but for whites as well. Learning about diversity was an educational imperative whatever the percentage of racial diversity at the institution itself. Moreover, by incorporating more diversity into the curriculum, the academic community as a whole came to see the value of diversifying not only the student body, but also the administrative staff and the faculty.

As important as diversifying the institution has proved to be in these nineteen projects, the best practices at institutions recognized the profound inaccuracy of reducing a person to a single, flattened, narrowly construed identity. Consequently, these institutions refused to be boxed into the limitations of "you need to be one to teach one." They avoided simplistic notions that any of us carry a single identity that should determine what one studies, whom one teaches, or which group one counsels. One of the most important lessons from Haverford College's diversity project was the value and the power of having a more empowered but knowledgeable professor from a dominant group teach subject matter about a marginalized group. Students in particular commented on the importance of having a Christian religion professor teach a course on anti-Semitism in the early Christian church. Similarly, students echoed sentiments about their male science professor who taught a course on gender and science.

Some of the Ford grantees in the South were particularly strong in integrating programs and curriculum designs that explored black–white issues. The intellectual and social challenge will be moving to the next stage in which other racial minorities are studied and a much more complex dynamic emerges. Currently diversity means race before it means anything else on most campuses, although gender follows closely behind. Class, a concept Americans like to pretend does not exist but which, in fact, has considerable influence in structuring lives and determining access to power and money, is rarely a well-defined part of diversity initiatives. Similarly, sexual orientation is infrequently addressed. When gay and lesbian issues are attended to, often its inclusion is the result of the composition of the student body, the geographic location of the college, or a tradition within a given institution of exploring a wide range of issues. Unless it is part of the definition or historical mission of the institution, religion is often overlooked as well. The same is true of other differences such as age or disability. Nonetheless, ultimately these layered and intertwined differences need to be integrated into a framework of analysis. Whatever the choice about what to include in a diversity course or program, it is important that there be thoughtful reasons for why a particular approach or definition has been adopted.

In some cases, institutions opted to adopt culture-specific perspectives such as Latin America or Africa, rather than focus on broader, more inclusive issues such as race, class, or gender. Such an approach relies on bringing in the experiences of different cultures without necessarily substantively altering the basic canon of the discipline. The danger of a culture-specific approach is that issues of power and discrimination can be avoided, although that is not always the case. Whatever the approach, it is important that dialogues about diversity eventually include broader systemic analyses of the sources and uses of power.

Different issues can become a lightning rod for conflict in diversity work. Race is the most typical one that generates controversy as it did at Tulane University, but at the University of Redlands it was gender that provoked strongly felt disagreements. At Brandeis University, it was religion that caused some Christians to feel dismissed, while at Haverford College it was Jewish students who sometimes felt erased by Christian practices. The very fact that there is such a deafening silence at some institutions about class or sexual orientation suggests that both are laden with such potential conflict that most schools chose not to address either one explicitly.

One area of development for the next generation of diversity projects is how to create for students in new diversity courses a sense of fundamental intellectual and personal engagement that faculty members as a rule seem to derive from the faculty seminars. While some students reported transformative changes as a result of the newly developed diversity courses, others were not only less engaged but also sometimes totally unaware that they were in a diversity course. In some cases, what engages faculty members might not engage students in the same way or with the same degree of enthusiasm. The faculty development seminar at Brandeis on integrating new scholarship about Africa and African oral traditions into the freshman humanities course that previously examined only ancient Greek culture was not, it turned out according to students interviewed, a particularly effective place for students to begin their exposure to diversity. Although the faculty teaching the courses were genuinely changed by the seminar experience, it was, students explained, too far removed to be a developmentally appropriate initiation for them into diversity. By contrast, students spoke with far more excitement about other diversity courses like "Race and Ethnicity in America" and "The Body and Disease" with which they could more immediately engage as an initial way in to questions diversity poses.

One of the several challenges of the coming decade's work on diversity, then, is how to sustain the commitment and energy so necessary to this enterprise. Are there a variety of places in the curriculum through which students can enter the debate and discover the value of diversity? Do these occur over time so the students can revisit some ideas and test their responses as they themselves mature and acquire greater intellectual capacities, confidence, and experience? How often must one course, an introductory one at that, or one upper-level capstone course taken late in a student's academic career carry the full burden of educating students about diversity? Is the curriculum the only place they will learn about diversity, or might they learn parallel or complementary or even conflicting ideas through other areas in the institution: through residence halls or lecture series, through student-sponsored cultural events or community service, through counseling and career centers, and through the diverse leadership evident in the administration and the faculty?

From the nineteen Ford-funded projects, a set of twelve principles did emerge as general guideposts that should help future programs create projects that can not only be sustained but also flourish. The dozen principles include the following and, if attended to, should enhance diversity projects in the immediate decade:

1. Engage as wide a group and as diverse a group as possible in the planning, implementation, and evaluation of diversity projects.
2. Tie the project into the mission of the institution and reflect it in as many areas as possible so there is a complementariness and a wholeness to it.
3. Consider the history, purpose, and historical moment of your specific institution as you design the project.
4. Be clear about the goals of the project and the audience you are trying to reach.
5. Take time to develop a well-conceived remedy for the problems your project is trying to solve.
6. Set goals you can achieve in the given time of a project.

Hold fast to the fact that addressing diversity issues
is important work for the academy, the nation, and
the world. It is socially urgent, intellectually
compelling, and personally transforming

7. Integrate both a short-term and a long-term vision. Since there is a
    built-in limitation to what one can do in a single grant of short dura-
    tion, it is best if it is integrated into the institution's long-range plans.

8. Embed assessment in your project at the outset and have clearly desig-
    nated people who are responsible for following through so that after the
    grant is over, you have some measure of the successes, next steps, and
    failures.

9. Have a strategy for institutionalizing the goals of the project in minor
    and major ways so there is a mechanism for completing unfinished work
    and assuring the continuity of accomplishments.

10. Use the project to help define the logical next steps for the institution.

11. Throughout the project, communicate regularly with a varied public in-
    ternally and externally so they can be better educated about the pur-
    poses and achievements and even the difficulties of your project. They
    can be allies and advocates in sustaining the project.

12. Hold fast to the fact that addressing diversity issues is important work
    for the academy, the nation, and the world. It is socially urgent, intellec-
    tually compelling, and personally transforming.

While faculty anguish over what kind of diversity requirement is appropriate, administrators struggle over how to integrate a holistic approach
to diversity on their campuses, and supporters of diversity initiatives try to
sustain their various projects, the task of living out the realities of diversity
goes on. People do it as best they can, which sometimes is with great pain
and sometimes with great courage, sometimes with impatience and other
times with unsettling serenity. This is true for minority staff as well as minority students. It holds as well for openly gay and lesbian people on campuses and for their colleagues who choose to remain closeted. It is true for
religious minorities whose customs and sacred holidays are ignored or whose
practices are mocked. It is true for all who wait and work for the day their
difference is acknowledged and understood even if it is not fully embraced.

Students in particular crave arenas in which to work out diversity
issues in practical, immediate ways. They need institutional support to help

them find these spaces not only in the classroom but also outside of its doors where students spend most of their lives. The next decade's work will, then, need to correct the self-defeating divide that exists on most campuses between student and academic affairs. We will need to integrate more consciously the work of the curriculum and the work of the cocurriculum. To achieve such cooperation across institutional areas of responsibility will require new institutional alignments between academic and non-academic areas in colleges and universities. We will need to invent new ways of working together and better structures that will make those collaborative efforts easier.

As we create more inclusive academic institutions, we need to keep in mind as we plan that differences are fluid, not static, multiple, not single. Each of us is a member of many different communities and most of us can claim several racial, ethnic, and/or religious heritages. We have both inherited communities and chosen ones. Frequently our communities don't intersect, interact, or even always like each other. The negotiating we must do on a daily, personal level is extraordinary. We each are a complex multicultural self in a world that allocates power and opportunities differently depending on what set of differences marks us. Staff members of color at one institution, for instance, were eloquent in explaining how they understood their identities as people of color and wanted to work with students of color to help them succeed in the academy. But they also wanted to be perceived as professionals, as the dean of student affairs, that is of *all* students, whatever their color. They wanted to be perceived as an academic dean who was also a woman, a mother, a daughter, a Ph.D. Pigeonholing into one narrow identity flattens out and, more importantly, misrepresents the complexity and reality of all our lives.

To create an institutional culture with institutional policies, structures, and practices that can embrace such simultaneity and complexity is indeed a humbling task. We can do no less, however, if we hope to create an academy that will teach people of today how to build a global society tomorrow free of violence, filled with variety, guided by respect for the living, and confident of our mutual interdependence for our mutual survival. At the end of several years of work, poised in most cases to continue additional diversity initiatives in some form, the nineteen Ford grantees realized that by turning to diversity, they learned something about how to create such an academy. Instead of a "problem," diversity became for them a blessing. In the words of the president of Spring Hill College, "Diversity is God's gift to the world." It remains to be seen what we will each do with such a treasure.

Notes

1. Renato Rosaldo, *Culture and Truth: The Remaking of Social Analysis* (Boston: Beacon Press, 1993), xvii.

2. Adrienne Rich quoted in Frances A. Maher and Mary Kay Thompson Tetreault's *The Feminist Classroom* (New York: Basic Books, 1994), 1.

3. References in this paragraph are taken from a February 8, 1990, letter from the Ford Foundation which was sent to the presidents of two hundred colleges and universities invited to submit proposals to the foundation's new Campus Diversity Initiative.

4. Allan Bloom, *The Closing of the American Mind* (New York: Simon and Schuster, 1987), 323.

5. Roberta M. Hall and Bernice R. Sandler, *The Classroom Climate: A Chilly One for Women?* (Washington, D.C.: Association of American Colleges, 1984).

6. The quotations in this paragraph and the one below are taken from the Ford Foundation letter to college presidents, February 8, 1990, cited in note 3 above.

7. Leslie Marmon Silko, *Ceremony* (New York: Penguin, 1977), 35–36.

8. References to quotations from faculty members, staff, and students emerged through personal interviews, correspondence, etc., during the course of the evaluation.

9. We are especially grateful to the conversation and preparatory notes compiled by Haverford College Professor Anne McGuire, who enumerated classroom climate and pedagogical issues that had been discussed in Haverford's faculty development seminars and which proved to be particularly significant in McGuire's Social Justice course, "The Origins of Christian Anti-Semitism." Quotations in this paragraph are from notes taken by a Ford Evaluator during a meeting at Haverford College with McGuire and several students who had taken her course.

10. From summary notes prepared by Haverford Professor Anne McGuire.

11. The quotation is taken from materials provided by Virginia Commonwealth University to the Ford Evaluator.

12. Benjamin R. Barber, "The Civic Mission of the University," in Richard M. Battistoni and Benjamin R. Barber's *Education for Democracy* (Dubuque: Kendall/Hunt Publishing, 1993), 453, 455.

13. This quotation emerged from an interview with a Ford Evaluator during a site visit to Spring Hill College.

14. This quotation is taken from files at the Ford Foundation.

15. From an evaluation form for Boundaries and Borderlands: The Search for Recognition and Community in America, a ten-day summer institute funded by the National Endowment for the Humanities and the Ford Foundation as part of the Association of American Colleges and Universities' American Commitment Curriculum and Faculty Development Project.

16. This quotation is from an interview with a Ford Evaluator during a site visit.

17. Ronald Takaki, *A Different Mirror: A History of Multicultural America* (Boston: Little, Brown and Company, 1993), 428.